'Just Say No'

To Bad Financial Advice

By

**Kevin Brunner &
Christian M Ramsey AIF ®**

'Just Say No'

To Bad Financial Advice
By Kevin Brunner & Christian M Ramsey AIF®

ISBN: 978-1-968149-04-8
Joint Venture Publishing
The Millionaire Mentor, Inc.

JMP
JOINT VENTURE

TABLE OF CONTENTS

Part 1 – JUST SAY NO!

Part 2 – CAPITAL GAINS TAX STRATEGIES

Part 3 – CASE STUDIES OF CAPITAL GAINS TAX STRATEGIES

TESTIMONIALS

Edward Carels

Ph.D. Acting CEO at Addiction Recovery Resources

"Kevin is a very astute expert on financial planning and investments. He prepares his recommendations clearly and with great precision."

Christopher Woo

Technology Consultant and Leader

"Kevin Brunner is the kind of financial manager and advisor you want to keep a secret, but only because you don't want to share his time or advice with anyone else. His approach is a breath of fresh air in a world of pushy, over-the-top salesmen. He knows his financial strategies are sound, can easily explain to even the most naïve of clients why his financial devices work, and then lets you make your own decisions. He's approachable, friendly and low-key. When you want to stop worrying about retirement, have a sit down with Kevin and put your mind at ease."

William "Bill" Craddick
Plant Manager

> "Kevin did a great job for me. He's a highly skilled professional. He worked diligently with me to get me on the right path."

Bruce Nelson
Real Estate Professional

> "Kevin is a pleasure to work with. My experience has found him to be highly conscientious and thorough with excellent follow up skills. I recommend Kevin for any business relationship that you may be pursuing."

Mario Nick Gallo
Commercial Real Estate Professional – Investments

> "I've known Kevin for years now and I would highly recommend Mr. Brunner for Wealth Management Strategies. I feel his experience owning and operated his own businesses aside from Brunner Financial has provides a very valuable and unique insight when working with clients as he can see their goals, issues, and objectives through their eyes allowing him to provide a strategic analysis, as well as, consultative and best practice recommendation for his high net worth individuals and family offices alike. I've further had the pleasure to see him perform in person
> through the many meetings we've been in and clients

we've worked with and as far back as my SoCal Real Estate days. If there is one professional with a stellar track record, acute business insights and cutting—edge Wealth Management Strategies, Kevin Brunner is him."

Neftali Fernandez

Real Estate Professional

"I had the pleasure of doing business with Kevin Brunner and was very impressed with his financial management knowledge. He presented very creative financial management plans and options to invest in innovative financial and insurance solutions to help you make wise decisions on your long—term goals."

Robert Medaris

Real Estate Professional

"During the time I have known Kevin he has displayed that he is a hard working person with ambitions to achieve his vision. His enthusiasm, commitment, and persistence are readily apparent. He values fairness and mutual success, which are valuable and enjoyable. I found Kevin
to be easy to work with and he very clearly explains the pros and cons to financial options that are available. I would have no problem recommending a conversation with Kevin regarding long terms and objectives, you will probably be very surprised and pleased."

Janey Tarpein
Senior Manager, Strategic Operations Implementation

"It's been a pleasure to work with and get to know Kevin. He is a hard-working individual whose ambition to achieve his vision, as well as his enthusiasm, commitment and persistence are readily apparent to all who meet him. He values fairness and mutual success, which makes for valuable and enjoyable long-term relationships."

Douglas Aloff
Real Estate Professional

"During the time I have known Kevin, I have known him to be a values-driven businessman with only the best interest of his customers and fellow business associates in mind. Kevin is a driven, high powered, well-educated individual that can truly make a difference in one's organization as well as an individual's personal growth. I would not hesitate to recommend Kevin in any business or personal venture."

Jeffrey Duvall
Operations Supply Chain Manager

"Kevin's demonstrated himself to be an expert in wealth planning and financial strategies. Kevin's approach is refreshing in that he operates with his customers' best interests in mind, and he takes the steps necessary to educate them. Kevin's sound value system, integrity, and expert knowledge make him a professional I'd recommend to others."

Michael Oldag

Development Engineer

"I have found Kevin to be easy to work with and he can clearly explain the pros and cons of the many financial options that are open to you. He can also offer innovative alternatives for your consideration which will help you get a better focus to make informed decisions on your long-term goals."

Rudy Murrieta

Project Manager

"Kevin is a Financial expert who thinks outside of the box. This enables him to obtain customers needs."

Chris Clark Sr.

Marketing Representative

"In my time working with and for Kevin, his hard work ethic was displayed in the long hours he put in at the office, as well as the research he conducted in order to provide the best strategy for his clients. Kevin has the ability to connect with a client because of his understanding of each individual client's needs. He has the ability to recommend financial strategies that align with their short-term cash flow needs and long-term financial goals. The thing I really like about Kevin is that he would rather sacrifice a high paying commission in order to provide a client with the best product. He is not a financial advisor, however, a strategist that helps build a client's wealth, as well as meet their retirement goals. His knowledge and experience allow him to build a retirement roadmap and advises the client along the way."

Andrei Poludnewycz

CEO, and Owner at JobCrank Inc.

"Kevin is an outstanding business and financial strategist. I was very impressed with his business background, knowledge and experience. He provided me with some excellent financial advice and guidance, which I believe will generate outstanding returns in the years ahead. I highly recommend Kevin to anyone in need of strong financial and/or retirement planning guidance."

William Newcomer

Manufacturing Plant Manager

"Kevin Is a true professional in the field of arbitrage strategies, with tax benefits on contributions, tax deferral during asset growth and tax benefits upon withdrawal and how these strategies can be used for business and personal growth. I strongly recommend him to anyone looking for solutions in dealing with Financial Strategies for a Tax-Efficient Retirement "

Mark Boersma

Owner, Synergy Solutions, Inc.

"Kevin's approach to partnering with other companies is very unique. He is all about helping his partners put systems in place which create a WIN WIN for everyone. The questions he asks are very interesting and make you think about yourself, your personality, your vision, and what you are looking for in a partnership. Very interesting and unique way of approaching business!"

Jason Pratt

Regional Operations Manager

"Kevin did an awesome job increasing my wealth, lowering my taxes and building my online business. We will certainly work together again."

Jameson Garrett

Senior Business Development Manager for Aerospace

"Kevin is the rare financial advisor who shows deep personal interest in his clients' specific circumstances and needs. He understands the market trends and how to optimize my investment portfolio to minimize risk and expenses, yet provide excellent returns. I know Kevin's primary motivation is his sincere concern about my financial success and his advice is always focused solely on my best interest."

James Evanow
Professional Speaker/Trainer, and Sea Captain

"Kevin Brunner is a top-notch financial strategist and insurance expert. I have had the pleasure of speaking with Kevin and he has stories and anecdotes that keep the crowd mesmerized. I highly recommend Kevin Brunner for any investment strategies that you may be pursuing in the future."

Steve Huang
MBA, Visual Communication Expert

"Kevin can explain the complex world of financial security in very simple and clear fashion. Moreover, he also has great ideas about how things should work. He is worth talking to just to learn about the industry."

Dave Peronto
Operations & Logistics Professional

"Kevin is an expert in his field putting his vast knowledge to work for the best interests of his clients. His years of experience and in-depth research put him at the top of his field. His friendly manner and common sense approach also make it easy to work with Kevin and understand his recommendations that will lead to a better financial future for his clients"

Daniela Bliss

Mortgage Consultant & Loan Officer

"I have had the pleasure in working closely with Kevin. I appreciate the networking relationship that we have. Kevin is a true professional that goes beyond the basic job requirements. He is caring and takes the time with clients to ensure they are educated and informed of their decisions. Kevin is very knowledgeable in his profession and is a believer of collaborative teamwork. A definite pleasure to work with. I will continue to recommend Kevin to my clients, knowing they are in good hands and will be well taken care of. I would recommend Kevin to anyone and look forward to working with him in the future!"

Rich Hall

Business Consultant and Investor

"I've had the opportunity to consult with Kevin Brunner regarding tax-free investments to benefit my family in retirement, as well as my heirs. He has developed a fantastic system that allows an investor to gain a better rate of return than other types of investments and to allow disbursements without a tax burden as well. I strongly recommend that you explore the program he has developed. I was very impressed with his intelligence and knowledge of investing, tax law and how to work the system to your own benefit."

Lyle Kan

Senior Vice President, Strategic Planning & Business Development

"Kevin understands his business and the products. He can easily explain how very complex financial products work. He does his homework and research before making any recommendations. I believe Kevin acts in the best interests of his clients."

Gary Metz

Vice President of International Operations

"Kevin is a straightforward, no-nonsense professional with boatloads of skills, abilities and experiences to share."

Bryan Whited MBA

PhD in Organization and Project Management

"Kevin is well versed in the financial industry and will do everything that he can to place his clients into their best financial position."

ABOUT THIS BOOK

This Book is the creation of Q Financial, and its purpose is to discuss a variety of financial topics philosophies, and fallacies while also addressing Q Financial's interpretation of the "Best of Breed" solution for Capital Gains Deferral Techniques; 'The Model Q™ Structured Installment Sale' and the CB Farmers Trust Delaware Statutory Trust Program'.

This eBook will not just talk about the Q Financial solutions, however...we will actually discuss every solution available in modern US Tax Law to address Capital Gains Tax and provide illustrations of each Technique.

"Model Q™'" is a major part of this eBook. Model Q™ is an interpretation of Income planning and Investment Allocation and was developed by Kevin Brunner of Q Financial and refined over many years. While the majority of this eBook is about Capital Gains deferral, reduction, and elimination...the broader message is actually about solving Income needs as part of a Lifetime Income plan and how these Capital Gains Deferral strategies can be best deployed to fit within those guidelines.

A Lifetime Income plan can take many shapes and use many tools, but understanding your options for utilizing available tax advantages is a tremendous force multiplier in terms of strategy effectiveness.

The term "tax-advantaged" as used by this eBook is mainly in reference to avoiding or deferring Capital Gains Tax, however many of these techniques also have estate or 'death tax' benefits as well and some will even address depreciation recapture.

There are many other ways to sell real estate or business property that are not covered by this eBook because of where they fit for the "Average Investor" (Average being not too poor and not too wealthy!). Offshore is not really covered, Opportunity Zones are not even mentioned except in this sentence and there are even other techniques that may be domicile or country or province-specific and require a specific structure of income classification and a bunch of fancy accounting.

This eBook also does not comment on those 'super-specific' and 'year-to-year' contractual techniques other than to acknowledge that they do exist.

It is safe to say that this eBook is all about keeping the most money one can when selling a highly appreciated asset using the best-known and widest available techniques.

Further, this eBook is of use to the average investor with assets up to around 20 million of net worth. If you have between $20 Million and $50 Million net worth you probably have your own highly paid professional team and can afford very customized strategies…but caution! Folks in that net worth bracket can just as easily lose everything on bad planning and bad advice.

Folks with over $50 million of net worth actually have to work hard to lose capital and are largely insulated from any sort of financial concern. It becomes more about keeping the wealth in the family at that level. This eBook is only of limited value to those individuals but may be of value to their extended family who may someday inherit significant assets.

This eBook is actually useful as a (hopefully!) easy-to-read primer for super affluent households and their extended family… for those families that are actively seeking knowledge on tools to control or have oversight or maintain meaningful negotiations to keep that wealth through the second and third generations (which only seems to happen about 40% for the second generation and about 5% of the time for third generation wealth according to the data!).

Finally, this eBook will only be of limited use to very low-income earners (except when capital gains recognition is structured to maintain government and state welfare programs!).

Now I should definitely mention that this eBook is not designed to be mathematically precise, nor is it designed to fully explore any of the topics of discussion. Rather a broad overview of each strategy is presented in plain English format with the absolute minimum of 'legalese'. Case studies are presented in story format to attempt to show the reader the intent and suggest the best use for each technique described.

Chapters are typically very short, between two to seven pages to purposefully hone in on the working components behind a given topic.

This means that a great deal of information is missing from each strategy discussed.

The intent is to create an easy-to-read dialogue of ideas that will hopefully give the reader a starting point in exploring their options for how the future sale of a business or property can tie directly into Income planning for potentially multiple generations.

...and of course, please keep in mind the purpose-built tools offered by Q Financial, the Model Q™ Structured Installment Sale (SIS), and the CB Farmers Delaware Statutory Trust (DSTP) programs. Q Financial believes them both to be the most transparent, elegant, and cost-effective techniques currently available to help craft a Lifetime Income plan and defer Capital Gains Tax in the safest ways possible.

FOREWORD BY KEVIN BRUNNER

From a very young age, I spent a great deal of time with my grandfather. He made me read books like "Think and Grow Rich" , "The Power of Positive Thinking", "The Richest Man in Babylon", "Poor Richard's Almanac", and "Thomas Payne" among others. Heavy reading for that age.

This formed my worldview.

I watched him closely and attended his meetings and business dealings, usually in Harry's Chinese restaurant, where after school I'd bus tables, wipe them down, take out the trash, and sometimes even help serve, all for tips. I was 9 to 14 years old. It was a different time, no one thought twice about a 9- year-old busing tables.

After a meeting, Grandpa would ask me questions about what was said and what I thought, and he'd explain things. He had several friends, who later after his passing I was also close to. They're all long gone now. Harry, was from Hong Kong, Jan was from Tel Aviv, and Grandpa was Swiss/American. A Christian, a Buddhist, and a Jew. Yes, it sounds like the start of a bad joke, '…walked into a bar.' And they told each other those jokes. They were terrible, but best of friends, always doing deals on a handshake, complete trust. Grandpa even learned some Cantonese and

Hebrew, and Harry learned some Swiss (never call someone from Switzerland or Swiss Language 'German', they will be greatly offended.)

Privately they'd tell me how much they each admired the other, but together it was often teasing.

I enjoyed the long conversations at the barber shop as well. I knew a lot of politics for a 9-year-old, but none of my friends understood Watergate, taxes, and local city council issues, I ended up with mostly grown men as friends. They never hesitated to answer my questions. Good men, family men, in a small town where your word was all you had.

I learned a great deal from them and other men like them. Out of respect always rise when a woman comes to or leaves the table, hold the door, mind your language when a woman is present, be kind, always tip the waitress and the barber, you always have time to stop and help with that flat tire, and never let the offering plate pass without giving something to it. Never judge a person for something they cannot control, like their color, or family. Never tell anyone when you have helped someone else. Never show off your wealth. Look a man in the eye, shake his hand, and keep your word.

It was a very fortunate childhood.

Those lessons are not lost, the wisdom shared was invaluable, I was able to tap lifetimes of experience. And I pray here to share as much of that, and everything learned since, with you. Learning never ends, or at least it shouldn't.

Grandpa said, 'When you don't get what you wanted, you got experience.' And 'It is better to learn from someone else's mistakes, than your own'. And 'Try to learn the lesson the first time'.

A lot of what he said was from Will Rodgers and Mark Twain, but wisdom all the same.

Our Purpose Here: In this eBook we are trying to address the big financial event, the sale of a business, the sale of real estate, and the day you retire. How to Maximize Income and Minimize Taxation.

Important things like a parachute, must work when needed. Traditional financial planning works in 2 out of 3 historical timelines, one of the 3 barely, and 1 of the 3 completely folds. Would you jump out of an airplane if your parachute opened only 2 out of 3 times?

Taking the safer approach, and managing taxes long term, actually provides you more net-net spendable income over the long term. Who knows, maybe you'll miss the adrenaline-fused nail-biting stress of watching the markets every day of your retirement. It is exhilarating when it goes up, the same as the Roulette Wheel when you win. Is that a retirement plan?

Talking to an advisor about those who were successful in the past may or may not help you going forward, Survivorship Bias. Wikipedia has an excellent explanation of this: The logical error of concentrating on entities that passed a selection process while overlooking those that did not.

The same strategy that worked in 1990–1999 didn't work in the early 1970s, 2000–2003, 2008–2009. The standard 60/40 and 4% income plan no longer works. Unless you had significantly more saved than you needed, it never really did.

Three things will make or break your retirement:

Sequence of Returns Risk, Taxes/Expenses, and Losses.

Your paradigm must be planning first for income, not chasing returns. Market up, market down, the bills come every month, life functions on income. 'Buy and hold' is for the young or the very wealthy and ends as a strategy when you are 10 years out from retirement. One market downcycle within that window, and you're working another 5–8 years. Two down cycles in a single decade, like the early 2000s and you may never retire.

Sequence of Returns Risk: Financial advisors use selective examples, and people look at those who are successful in investing in the stock market and have no idea it is most often Survivorship Bias.

Just because somebody once flipped a quarter 10 times and got heads 10 times in a row doesn't mean it's a good strategy or he's the best 'quarter flipper'. Financial advisors (mostly the brokers above them) most often pick those that work out well, selective examples. Show me the outcome you want, and we can design a study to prove it. Survivorship Bias.

What percentage of the 60/40 Stocks/Bonds Model with the 4% income rule, does it actually work out, depending on the year range selected, is often less than half. It most often fails when you start taking income. But wasn't replacing income the whole point of saving and investing?

When given an example, ask to demonstrate it again, only change the sequence, can it be duplicated without being selective in the data? And they trail off in lengthy legal jargon about 'past performance is not a guarantee of potential or future performance', although true, it and other phrases are designed by lawyers to keep accountability or liability away from those we are relying on for just that, accountability.

It doesn't matter that the model of Modern Portfolio Theory has failed to perform for three decades. The Nobel Prize-winning author of the theory Harry Markowitz later disavowed the strategy as it no longer works (look it up). Still, it is a staple of financial advisors because they've got nothing else to offer. At least nothing the broker that holds their license will allow them to promote to clients. (because the broker makes less money if you follow other strategies)

If you were to retire for example in a market upswing like 1997-99, or 2005-07, within 3 years you were either returning to work (think Home Depot or Walmart Greeters) or drastically scaling back your retirement, or 'downsizing' to a Florida senior condo complex. And the Reverse Mortgage business is booming.

And these market cycles come often, every 8-12 years or so, it's no surprise, we know this.

Modern Portfolio Theory, the 60/40 Stocks/Bonds Model, and the 4% Income Rule, all have dramatically failed at least three times in the last 30 years. All due to something beyond any of our control; Sequence of Returns Risk.

Sequence of Returns; you cannot control it, but you can plan for it and hedge against it. How do you deal with that as a Financial Advisor? This is where Model Q™ comes from.

Taxes/Expenses: Next comes controlling expenses, and not just the advisory fees. Taxes are your greatest expense. If not managed well, taxes will eat not only 30% of your retirement savings but eat the compound returns those lost taxes will never earn again.

Do you believe taxes in 10 or 20 years will be higher or lower?

Taxes and tax laws are often a shell game. When Ronald Reagan, later George W Bush, lowered the marginal tax rates, they also took away deductions or reduced them. The effective tax paid by the average citizen actually increased. After all, they needed to feed the Military Industrial Complex to defeat the Soviets, the Chinese, the terrorists, and the Russians, but mostly to feed their campaign donors and relative's stock options. The psychology of the lower Marginal Rates worked, and people spent (and the Federal Reserve printing presses were in high gear) and drove the economy up, even though the effective taxes paid increased. This wasn't only trickle-down economics; it was a shell game.

We are paying more taxes now than we ever have. Read '151 taxes in a loaf of bread'. You paid your 'fair share' every trip to the grocery store. You must control expenses – taxes are an expense that can and must be managed. Once you send in those taxes, those dollars will never be working for you again. That's a loss.

Buying Minibonds is not the solution, and a Roth IRA is something we all should have, but not the only solution either. You must think in terms of Net-Net spendable income. What am I left with to buy groceries, utilities, medical expenses, travel, and gifts for the grandkids?

Your Advisor or CPA are likely not having those conversations with you. If you are only deferring your taxes it's not enough. Sometimes paying the tax is better than deferring. Sometimes deferring is better. Tax elimination is best. We cannot escape income taxes altogether. In practice, it's usually a nuanced blend with ongoing adjustments along the way.

Losses: Controlling for losses is the easiest part, and most advisors are way too willing to accept risk with your money. Losses happen; without some risk the reward is very low. But you can control for risk, and the best vehicles for this are hated by most advisors (actually their broker bosses hate them) Dave Ramsey and Clark Howard hate them too. The latter two have often promoted disinformation about these financial instruments, I believe knowingly, and in the case of Ramsey for self-interest (His business model, how he really gets paid, is generating leads for advisors that sell mutual funds and term insurance).

Focusing on the worst of an overall winning investment sector is not evidence all of them are bad investments.

When you're in the top 0.05% of the population's average income and can live in luxury on 20% of your annual gains, your strategy doesn't work for the remaining 99.5%.

Back to Survivorship Bias, it influences many things. An example provided means it was successful for the group selected, nothing more. If you are to analyze what is the most successful way to save for retirement you must account for market timing which is the Sequence of Returns Risk, and expenses, especially taxes, and control for losses.

That's it. Model Q™

FOREWORD BY CHRISTIAN RAMSEY

When working with clients, I have often found that little or no attention is paid to transactions that often involve hundreds of thousands of dollars. Many times I have witnessed clients and friends using what I would consider to be "Tried and True" techniques that are not the best approach to realize their goals but are what they have heard of, and even when they go smoothly...there can be tax related surprises that are humbling very fast.

I have personally helped many people avoid or defer paying taxes when selling a property or a business. The average savings is always hundreds of thousands of dollars. Dollars that remain in your pocket, generating income according to the schedule you establish and paying taxes in whatever fashion best suits your long-term goals.

As a financial planner, estate planner, and investment advisor, my core competencies revolve around asset management and planning for clients throughout all stages of their lives. It is important to note how the sale of a property or business overlaps with the financial and estate planning arena and why I choose to be familiar with the process.

Financial planners, among other things, train very hard

to help a client transition from the accumulation phase to the preservation phase. This is the formal way of saying that there is a period in everyone's life when they are earning money through work and somewhere the line crosses over to where a person "reaps what they have sown". In other words, a person transitions to retirement or having their assets paid to them instead of an employer or a business.

There are many things to plan for during retirement and here is a quick overview of how it looks. Pensions and IRAs or 401k plans are supposed to cover about 60% of your retirement income. Social Security is projected to cover about 10%. About 30% of retirement (or replacement) income comes from "Other Assets".

Now the term "Other Assets" covers items like property or business interests, inheritance, royalties, and the like.

While we are discussing retirement income, it is very important to mention that there are only three ways to have an asset or an income in modern society.

1.) Tax Free
2.) Tax Deferred
3.) Taxable

The category of "Other Assets" is almost always fully taxable, while the remaining sources of retirement income are tax-advantaged to some degree.

Clients with appreciated properties or clients owning a business to some degree need to have knowledge of the tools that can help them manage taxation for a category of retirement income that can account for 30% (frequently more!) of how they support themselves through retirement.

This eBook is therefore about the long-term benefits of deferring or avoiding as much tax as possible as part of a "life plan". That is in part why this eBook hopes to show how a reader's personal life plan can be impacted by superior planning and education.

The best life plans and exit strategies borrow expertise from a number of disciplines and it is important to note that you should always consult with competent legal and tax advisors for advice specific to your scenario.

INCOME PLANNING – All About Model Q™

Before we really dive into Capital Gains Tax deferral techniques like the 1031 Exchange or Installment Sales or the Model Q™ Installment Sale Trust marketed by Q Financial, or the Farmland and Agricultural specific programs also available through Q Financial from CB Farmers Trust we want to spend some time changing the question you asked that caused you to get this eBook in the first place.

You probably asked for an eBook about "Capital Gains Tax advantages"...but we want to rephrase that question right off the bat and then change your entire paradigm.

You missed a step. It is NOT all about Tax Planning or Capital Gains Tax strategies.

It is really all about the Income. How to solve for Income needs first and then Invest for profits. We call this Model Q™ and it is important enough to be a Trademark of Q Financial. You will quickly see this is a significant portion of each of the Q Financial programs explained in this eBook. Model Q™ is actually the fundamental basis for WHY each strategy is effective in addressing Lifetime Income and applicable tax-advantaged techniques.

Kevin Brunner and Christian Ramsey met in 2016 after talking about Private Annuity Trusts and Deferred Sales

Trusts and specialty Charitable Trust Structures that were all fairly complex and really needed provable intent. Actually, Brunner and Ramsey really dived into the specific failure points of each technique and how the IRS would close 'loopholes' over time, issue warnings for "Promoters", disallow transactions, and more.

Really what happened was that two Industry Specialists with over a decade of experience each had come together for a "Meeting of the Minds".

Mr. Brunner was a Forbes Advisor of the Year, Military Veteran, and Defense Contractor and had successfully owned a Mergers and Acquisitions Company. Mr. Ramsey had published a Capital Gains strategy book, "Land Rich, Cash Poor" and had been a paid Continuing Education Provider for over six years for a curriculum based on that subject matter for organizations such as the CA Department of Real Estate, Northern CA CCIM Chapters, Association of Commercial Real Estate (ACRE), and Commercial Real Estate Women (CREW) and BOMA, NARPM and several title companies.

When Mr. Brunner reviewed the original copy of "Land Rich Cash Poor" from 2006, one of the first things he said was that he would have preferred a chapter dedicated to Income planning, and after some lively discussion, both professionals came together to help create Mr. Brunner's vision of Model Q™.

A craftsman gets to the point where he knows the work and

can perform every function flawlessly. What happens next is a period of efficiency. Steps taken to perform a task are questioned, examined, and may be changed somewhat to have a slightly different approach that adds percentages of value in time saved or quality. This process creates a master craftsman from a skilled journeyman.

I think this best represents the concept of Income planning as a higher form, or at least a different form and focus of formal Financial Planning as determined by the CFP (tm) Board of Standards.

Financial Planning and Estate Planning are largely based on trigger events (something you will learn more about in later chapters of this eBook) and accounting in some measurable way for what is best described as side roads and alternate routes on your retirement roadmap. A series of "If – Then" statements if you will, that are designed to formally uncover and address potential weaknesses. Financial Planning is really all about contingency awareness and how to measure harder-to-define circumstances.

Income planning, however, takes a shortcut and keeps to Brass Tacks. The nature of Income planning is all about the predictability of one of the most important aspects of retirement...a steady paycheck. Income planning overweighs the nature of predictable, lifetime income rather than the tools specifically used to create that lifetime income. We define Income planning as accounting for predictable income streams rather than really drilling down into the metrics of Bond Laddering as an example. First one ties down the income needed, and then one invests.

There is value to this approach. and, as Kevin Brunner explained it is all based on one simple question. "If the Stock Market tanked as it did in 2009-2010, and you suffered a 40% or greater loss in value of your Retirement nest egg. WOULD THAT IMPACT YOUR RETIREMENT INCOME?"

It is a simple question that efficiently and eloquently describes the value and paradigm shift of Income planning over other disciplines. It is the Elephant in the Closet, the Sumo Wrestler, and not the Ju Jitsu Master. Financial and Estate Planning and Investment Management are all tools that really support and improve Income planning. but without the Income, everything else loses value.

So, what, exactly is Income planning in practice? According to Mr. Brunner, a good starting point is roughly accounting for your Age in Income-Producing assets and only "Investing" with the difference. This kind of sounds familiar to a lot of folks, but do not get confused, because we are approaching the concept from Income planning specifically, so the connotation is quite different than what you think you may have heard before.

Normally this Age-In-Income preliminary recommendation comes from an idiom known as the "Wall Street Rule of Thumb" or the "Investment Rule of Thumb" and offers nearly the same advice. That advice is to have your Age allocated to

Bonds, Fixed Income Instruments, or Savings accounts and it relates to Investment Management and Asset Allocation for risk tolerance. (something also covered in greater detail in further chapters of this book). What this recommendation does is that it keeps your money invested...and that is where that elegant question comes into play. "If the Stock Market Tanked and your Portfolio took a 40% or Greater Loss, WOULD THAT IMPACT YOUR RETIREMENT INCOME.?"

It is a pesky and persistent question, isn't it?

So, the difference between Model Q™ and various rule-of-thumb systems for allocations lies in Systemic vs Non-Systemic risk. Income planning accounts for Systemic Risk in a way that the "Wall Street Rule of Thumb" does not. That is the core difference.

We would like to change your paradigm. This eBook is really all about Income planning and how managing gains taxes correctly really shows its colors to improve the Income planning process.

In other words, Let's talk about Model Q™ as an Investment Philosophy first! Then we will cover the best tax efficient Tools designed to improve the efficiency of Model Q™ when selling a highly appreciated Asset or Business to create Lifetime Income.

So, the Paradigm shift to consider is "What is your Income plan?" and then we start getting to how each Tax

Advantaged Strategy works with your Income plan according to Model Q™.

Instead of allocating to Investment Assets that are subject to risk, Income planning allocates those assets to predictable, repeat income sources first...and favors guaranteed income tools like annuities and lifetime income contracts and backup income tools like Hybrid Life Insurance policies and Real Estate and similar income-producing assets or business that maybe are not guaranteed or 100% Structured, but are still largely reliable.

If you are 65 years old and have $1 Million dollars in your retirement account, at the risk of a blanket recommendation when you begin Income planning, at least $650,000 of your money should go into a guaranteed income tool and be taken completely out of the Market and any Risk if there are no other considerations at play. This approach would favor predictable income and very low risk.

The remaining $350,000 is perhaps still worth speculating on unless a 40% or greater loss in value would impact your retirement income...in that case, a higher allocation might be reasonably assigned toward Income planning.

Now whenever you say something like "Guaranteed" and "Income" in the same sentence, you are usually talking about some form of an annuity. The formal definition of an annuity is "a series of substantially equal, periodic payments" and to get a "Guaranteed Income", well, you can only have a guarantee from an insurance company, so yes, we are talking about using an annuity to lock in as much income as can be done according to the Model Q™ version of Income planning.

Critics might make a blanket suggestion that annuities are expensive and that this version of Income planning does not account for purchasing power inflation or other performance metrics, they may also suggest historical average returns and "smooth out" loss years over time... such as "Return to Mean", and then mention 'Dollar Cost Averaging' and 'Long Term Buy and Hold' – these are all tricky fallacies if you will permit an author's opinion when accompanied by several observations of fact presented later in the Market Fallacies chapter.

This eBook will explain the pros and cons of each blanket recommendation in an apples-to-apples fair and balanced fashion that explores both the positive and negative consequences of each of those older philosophies.

That pesky question though...is still pertinent and absolutely needs to be asked before effective fine-tuning of a portfolio and retirement plan can occur.

"If your portfolio hits a 40% or greater loss year, will that impact your retirement? Will you need to cut back your withdrawals? Can you afford to trust that your balance will come back ...while you are taking your withdrawals during down years and being forced to take losses on positions because you can't wait for the position to be sold at a gain? "

Don't get me wrong, some folks with significant assets can actually lose 50% of their portfolio and it will not affect their lifestyle at all. That doesn't mean they WANT to lose 50% or that they look for loss positions in any way...if just means that maybe they can wait for a market upswing and recapture some losses and maybe get a few percentages points extra return for their trouble. It also means that their Income planning is already dialed down and that their money subject to market loss is appropriate.

The metric does not always work for the Affluent as a starting point...but then again, maybe it should be applied...I mean how many Lottery winners and Professional Athletes get Millions of dollars of net worth and yet file for bankruptcy soon thereafter? Well, the answer is obvious, a lot, most even, and all because they did not perform adequate Income planning...they just invested (or spent) their money.

Investments will always work until they do not. The purpose of the investment is usually to make money or to help with retirement. Both of these reasons are really talking about Income planning before Investing.

Every professional Real Estate investor has experienced a bad property. Every Business owner has experienced a bad deal. When you are talking about a lifetime Income plan one really needs to take as much risk as possible off the table. That is what Model Q™ does.

Model Q™ doesn't want and actually cannot afford ANY bad deals. Model Q™ wants guarantees first and foremost...then Model Q™ can get speculative!

Without Income planning, nothing else can easily fall into place. Asking that pesky question will help shape a positive outcome and yet still beautifully addresses the original concept of "Land Rich, Cash Poor" which is how to translate a Highly Appreciated Asset such as Real Estate or a Business into income for retirement while controlling the tax implication.

Investment Property Owners and Business Owners alike, already know about Income planning. That is exactly what they have already been doing intuitively to get successful... and the common issue that will always arise with Investment Property and a Business is that eventually, you cannot run it any longer or you are forced to sell.

You will, however, want the income to continue (or even increase) as you sell and transition to retirement and a different form of passive income.

INCOME PLANNING CASE STUDY

Let's work through a simple case study on Income planning.

David and Diane are both 55 and are thinking about retiring early after successful careers. David in equipment sales and Diane with the State. They have 2 kids, both in college and the kids are lucky enough to be satisfying their own educational requirements without leaning on Mom and Dad. David and Diane have a smaller home that is nearly paid for and has minimal debt. Over the last 30 years, David has managed to accumulate a 401k plan with just about $900,000 in it, and Diane has a 30-year State Pension that she can claim income from a normal retirement age (65) and has a smaller 457/TSP Plan with $250,000 in it.

The idea behind Income planning for this couple suggests that 50%-60% of their entire retirement assets be dedicated to some form of Guaranteed, Low-Risk Income-Producing tools, and taken completely out of the "Investment" bucket. What would $600,000 generate in terms of Lifetime guaranteed income? In today's environment probably close to $20,000/yr, or roughly 4% without running much of a risk of capital depletion. This leaves approximately $500,000 currently invested in the market and possibly earning money, possibly subject to market risk. The key with this scenario is Diane's pension doesn't kick in for 10 more years, but when it does, it will start at $50,000/yr., which means that David and Diane will presumably have at least $20,000 extra coming in on top of the pension award for normal retirement.

Early retirement, however, shows a large income gap unless more assets are used to secure income. $1.1 Million may be able to come very close to kicking out $50,000 a year in come for a long period of time, assuming David and Diane can live a fun retirement on $50,000 a year. If a fun retirement means an additional $15,000 in travel expenses every year for 10 years until age 65, there are tools to lock down that Income Need.

The Short answer for David and Diane is that they may actually be able to perform an early and modest retirement at age 55 due to Rule 72T which will allow for early withdrawals from their retirement accounts without a penalty. This is because their assumed Income Needs are not out of line with their retirement assets to produce income.

Now if David and Diane do their early retirement and do not address their income needs by proper Income planning, and their combined portfolio of $1.1 Million gets a 40% loss, such as what occurred in 2009, that leaves them with approximately $700,000. Does that severely impact their Retirement Income? You bet it does! The entire amount of $700,000 dedicated to income may only present $30,000 a year in predictable and reliable income... which takes early retirement clearly off the table. Buy and Hold investors from 2009 were roughly made whole after 5 years or recovery...that is too long to wait just to get back to Square 1 and it is entirely preventable by doing the necessary Income planning when retirement gets closer.

Do not risk what you do not need to. Plan your Income first and then Plan your investments. Make the best and most practical investments you can and use the most efficient money management systems you can. Speculate wisely. You will find it far more rewarding knowing that even if your investments nosedive unexpectedly, your retirement income has already been addressed.

MARKET FALLACIES :

Now that Q Financial has hopefully changed your paradigm about Income planning first and then Tax Planning… let's take a look at some other market Gotchas and apply some critical thinking to different sorts of professional financial services and their drawbacks.

PART

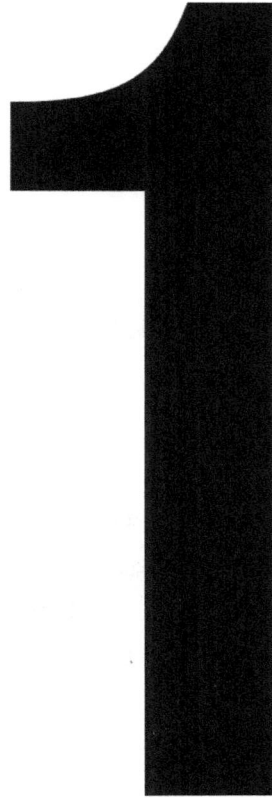

"Just Say No"

All About Market Fallacies

JUST SAY NO TO WOO-WOO NUMBERS!
The Tricky Landscape of Average Annual Returns

First off, Average Annual Return can be calculated in several ways and yet yield widely different results. Emphasis added quite on purpose. Please take an extra moment to digest that statement. This is, or it should be, a fairly well-known effect. Yet for some reason few understand and fewer still actively communicate exactly how much variance can occur by changing your method for return calculations.

It's sneaky.

You can have average annual returns calculated by date by cycle by an average of dates or cycles like point to point. Each calculation method will result in a greatly different cash balance which is largely dependent upon the amount of drawdown or negative losses that can occur during the accounting.

Sometimes this math trick is called the hidden cost of volatility, or the mathematics of declines and advances. How you choose to calculate the Average Annual Return slides right into that math trick!

What it means and incidentally how one can distinguish a professionally trained planner from a sales guy is that one can quite often have a very low rate of return that is consistent and when one compares that with a much higher variable rate of return, the cash balance tells the difference.

As an example, approximately 5 1/2 % earned every year consistently with no drawdown years and no loss years will generally have a double cash balance at the end of a 10-year cycle (not factored for Taxes or Expenses- just basics are referenced). This effect is also seen with the rule of 72 which suggests that you actually need a 7% return to achieve the same results if you have both positive and negative years over the same period.

Math can be tricky huh? To make it worse, and as a reminder, this eBook is not mathematically precise…but the relationship between calculable factors is what this eBook seeks to point out, not the actual formulas that you are welcome to look up. So for this model…we take the average annual return and during each period, take the one extra step to actually adjust the working cash balance per period and work it long form, by hand and not through the shortcut approximation for the entire term that is known as the Rule of 72.

That simple extra step of working the math by hand, per period, creates the divergence between what you think you see and what shows up on paper.

You always just look at the statement of cash value, right? Most investors do!

Keep looking at the cash value. That is your True metric and not necessarily the accepted calculation of one of the many variants of Average Annual Return.

The Rate of Return can be a deceptive metric of the Cash Balance results… This feeds directly into Buy and Hold and Return to the Mean, not really addressing portfolio risk in the same fashion that Income planning does.

This is also a glaring failure point of most off-the-shelf software and online tools available to Investment Professionals and the reason that hand calculations will never go out of style for accurate measurement.

This seemingly simple point of difference regarding the very basics of how to calculate Average Annual Return all by itself is actually a critical piece of Model Q™ and WHY it works better. When solving for income first… average annual return becomes a secondary qualification to drive the required Cash Balance needed to make those cash payments either Guaranteed or Structured.

If you only solve for a Rate of Return…well, you can get that rate and still fall short on cash needed to satisfy income needed. Woopsie! But it is 100% true. Especially if expenses and tax consequences are factored in.

Model Q™ applies the math in a way that the investor naturally notices the change in values on a statement.

Simple, right? And yet this is probably news to you, even if you are a Financial Professional. We encourage you to look up the formula and work the numbers by hand in a few different ways. You will quickly see the difference.

They used to call this "The Proof is in the Pudding." Meaning don't hide behind a nebulous calculation, cash balance and income need to be solidly accounted for, especially when you employ Model Q™ and solve for Lifetime Income planning first!

The next page shows a chart of four different investments. Look carefully at the three-year returns calculated and imagine how great the potential cash balance divergence becomes after twenty years! Now look at the effect of a big loss at the beginning vs the end of the term. Finally... look at the benefit of zero loss years and true compounded returns.

What do you think of Investment #4? No Loss Years and a Consistent Positive Return? It does not look flashy, but it is very high compared to the other similar and absolutely 'suitable' investments – more on that later!

Again - The following chart shows results only after Three Years!

$100,000 Start Balance	Investment 1	Investment 2	Investment 3	Investment 4
Yr 1 Return	0.2	-20%	0%	0.05
Yr 1 Balance	$120,000	$80,000	$100,000	$105,000
Yr 2 Return	-20%	0.1	0.35	0.05
Yr 2 Balance	$96,000	$88,000	$135,000	$110,250
Yr 3 Return	0.15	0.25	-20%	0.05
Yr 3 Balance	$110,400	$110,000	$108,000	$115,762
Total Return	0.15	0.15	0.15	0.15
Average Annual Return	5%	5%	5%	5%
Return on Investment	0.104	0.1	0.08	0.157
End Balance	$110,400	$110,000	$108,000	$115,762

The cash balance results are shocking enough to wonder why the definition of Average Annual Return is used at all for describing an investment, and yet it is. Even worse... one can actually have a positive Average Annual Return and yet have a decline in cash value over a period of time when factoring tax liability on the gains, especially with highly volatile positions experiencing big losses at the end of a term calculation.

Now that is some tricky math indeed!

JUST SAY NO TO BAD FINANCIAL ADVICE!

Understanding Risk and Diversification and Asset Allocation!

Capital at risk has several different accepted definitions, for our purpose of Income planning, capital at risk is generally much lower than the amount actually invested to achieve market-linked returns. In Model Q™, capital at risk is what is invested after the Income planning has been accounted for. Remember- Model Q™ favors income assets completely outside of market risk and largely, if not entirely reliable.

Literally every other technique you have heard has a Capital at Risk of virtually your entire Investment portfolio or 95% or higher. Here is where it pays to really know and understand the difference between Systemic Risk and Non-Systemic Risk.

Systemic Risk can look like 1) a Natural Disaster / Terrorist Attack preventing trading 2) a Blackout preventing trading 3) Market Disruption where the market is closed due to compounding algorithmic failure or major data feeds become corrupted or damaged.

If you can not trade, you can not buy and you can not sell. Orders get held or canceled. If you can not place a trade to get the cash, there is no deposit in your bank.

This is one form of Systemic Risk…but there are other descriptions of slightly different Systemic events that affect the Markets broadly and not just the mechanics of Trade!

Non-Systemic Risk would be any small-scale disruption or trade imbalance…like the recently noticed reliance upon Chinese imports for Medicine, Pharmaceuticals, or Personal Protection Equipment (PPE). The supply disruptions could cause a market imbalance or opportunity for gains and losses…but there is still a market, and you can still access your investments.

One type or risk cannot be protected by diversification. The other risk can absolutely be addressed by remaining invested in the market (100% Commitment or 100% Capital at Risk!) by simply being diversified in your investment allocation.

This means our Risk-Adjusted Return metrics (Sharpe or Traynor Ratios) for Model Q™ with less Capital at Risk have very high return potential for the amount of risk taken, it also means the potential return can be greatly reduced through reduced exposure. (Note: Model Q™ Solves for Lifetime Income first and THEN Invests!)

The spread of guaranteed return vs potential return can be fairly narrow, which offers significant planning advantages for both Income planning and Estate Planning strategies that favor predictable values yet still require some flavor of 'risk'.

This is also a contributing piece of Model Q™, without all of the fancy definitions.

Sometimes this eBook may get heavy in terms of technical, that is so the CPAs, Attorneys, and other Professionals that may read this book have some insight into the deeper functions of Model Q™ as an indication of Q Financial's philosophy.

Estate Planners often enjoy mostly predictable values or growth with some element of risk for Allowable Discounting as an example. Vegas Casinos certainly prefer VERY

predictable risk. When we use higher-level jargon in this eBook, we will do our best to present the intent and effect in plain English.

JUST SAY NO to More Bad Advice! The Changing Landscape of Diversification and Asset Allocation!

Q Financial believes Asset Allocation is dangerously close to being a market fallacy!

Let's reference a very interesting study from the late

1980s called the Brinson Hood Bebower study. Commonly called the BHB study and even though this is an eBook and does not require footnotes, the BHB study and both its supporting evidence and critical essays should be required reading for every investment professional as well as the Department of Labor and various Ethics Committees.

The subject matter of the BHB is highly contentious and seems to border on a marketing scheme rather than a provable result. In fact, it appears as if the BHB study helped to create the advancement of Mutual Funds as an investment product in the 1980s. Without the BHB study and the impact of its findings, the Investment World today would be very different indeed.

The moving parts of the BHB study suggest that there are three components to a successful portfolio.

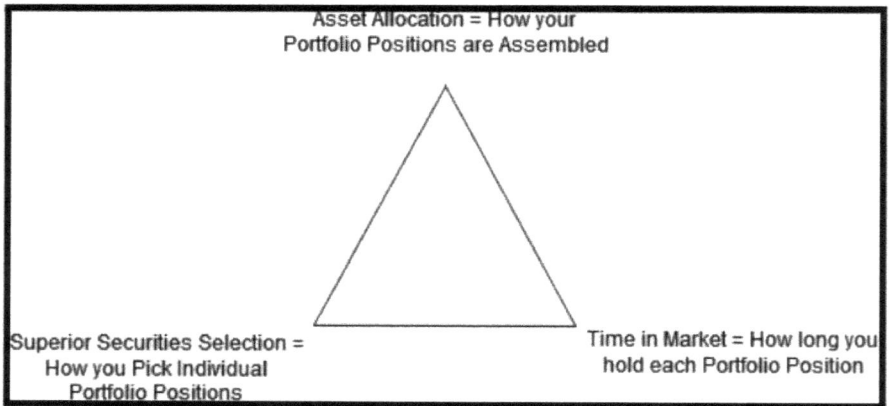

Asset Allocation = How your Portfolio Positions are Assembled

Superior Securities Selection = How you Pick Individual Portfolio Positions

Time in Market = How long you hold each Portfolio Position

The first would be superior security selection. Superior securities selection is a fancy word for what you pick as your investment, IE… what is your 'direct selection'.

The second component of a successful portfolio would be the asset allocation. Asset allocation in this context refers to how many superior selected products you designate for your allocation. What is your methodology? Your methodology determines your asset allocation. Do you only pick Stocks? Do you pick Stocks and Bonds? Do you pick Stocks and Bonds from the US Only or do you use Foreign Stocks and Bonds? Do you pick only ETFs (Exchange Traded Funds) or do you pick Mutual Funds? How many do you pick together? Is there a Sector or Industry you focus on?

These questions all drive the end result of your Allocation!

The third component of a successful portfolio involves market timing or time in the market. In this context what this means is how long you decide to hold each of your selected securities. IE when do you buy and when do you sell to create your asset allocation? What is your look-back period? What is your minimum Hold period? Does your custodian have Active Trading tests? Market Timing or Time in the Market refers directly to what causes you to change and re-evaluate your Allocation model.

So- depending on who you talk to how the math is employed and how the study is interpreted, one will find that the

Three Components of a successful Investment Portfolio as researched through the BHB study are grossly overweighted either towards Asset Allocation or Against Asset Allocation.

Let's rephrase that statement in a slightly different way…over 93% of projections are attributed either TO or AGAINST Asset Allocation based on the interpretation of the BHB Study.

Sometimes one really has to love how research language can be interpreted when one seeks to replicate the math of a finding!

We are actually going to explain how you can be 93% for or against the exact same mathematical findings and be correct each way!

So, depending on who you talk to, it can be determined that the most effective Portfolio over a given period of time is either almost always because of diversification or almost always because of lack of diversification.

Did the Investor only Invest in Microsoft for their entire life starting in 1990, or did the investor only invest in Kmart for their entire life starting in 1990? One was wildly successful, and one was a great failure.

Or…did the Investor only invest in S&P 500 stocks for their entire life starting in 1990?

This is the plain English rough interpretation of the data from the BHB study, and it suggests that unless you are very lucky with a Superior Securities Selection, then being diversified really is a great answer for long-term growth.

The Financial Industry, as a majority, seems to really take a third position slightly outside of the BHB Study results…be 95% to 100% Invested for your entire life and then be diversified. The Mutual Fund industry was born on the need for being diversified, even if you didn't have enough money to buy each stock individually, the smaller investor could buy a fund of multiple stocks and bonds with amounts as low as $25 and presto!... instant diversification!

So, $25 dollars of a Mutual Fund in 2012 vs $25 of Bitcoin in 2012 yields vastly different results…however, neither address investing in precisely the same way that Model Q™ does!

The picture becomes clearer when one realizes that the BHB study was widely touted by Fund Companies in the 80s for retirement plans to address that very "need". Back in those days, your company 401k Plan would only have one to three mutual funds available or even only a savings account. Diversification was fairly low, but that has evolved exponentially in modern markets so that position overlap is a research sub-industry all by itself!

So, the BHB study really created the Mutual Fund industry that we know today, where an Investor can and should buy a static allocation model for a longer-term investment position. That is directly the borderline fallacy that Q Financial would like to call to your attention.

Problems are always related to maintaining that static allocation model...investors don't tend to notice those issues. Even after Elliot Spitzer successfully brought many of those issues to light nearly twenty years ago like the hidden trading costs of Mutual Funds as well as the bucket of marketing expenses charged by Mutual Funds.

Now asset allocation is a manufactured product in the securities industry today and it involves quite a few additional red herring, client-beware situations than just being in a static model.

Probably the worst is a managed allocation model for a fee. Large brand name firms are notorious for offering an asset allocation service as a managed account which will reallocate your positions once a quarter for a fee typically around 1% when this is also basically a free service with modern allocation forward instructions.

Dipping in the cookie jar for extra cookies is a huge issue with nearly every brand name firm it seems like!

This is a prime example, and it is actually legislated against for most Retirement accounts at this point, but not for most Investment accounts and not for most Trust accounts. The Financial Industry actually fights very hard to maintain profitability at the expense of the Investor's benefit!

The Quarterly Rebalancing Allocation Service is actually free nine times out of 10 unless you go to a brand name firm. Please be extra careful that your management service is not simply a passive reallocation service!

Some of the less tedious but still concerning asset allocation systems are only involved with changing your allocation based on your age. So another caveat would be Age Based Allocations. What this means is that as you get older, your advisor's managed account will automatically adjust your risk out of the stock market and more heavily into the bond market. Again— this can be free with forward Allocation instructions and about 5 minutes of extra work for a client or Advisor to establish. Let's pretend not to mention that this age-based investment idea is really what your financial advisor should be doing already and not for any 'extra fees'— that is merely moving from one suitable investment to a somehow more suitable investment the next year or so simply based on your age and not the investment itself. More on suitable investments later!

The bottom line is that these lifestyle-type investments or 'age-weighted managed accounts' are inelegant and quite cheesy for what they actually DO yet they still charge the client 1% or more in extra fees.

This really is the work your advisor is supposed to do

for you automatically!

Model Q™ finds that the only managed account system actually worth having when solving for Income or Cash Balance Requirements is some form of actively managed account.

An actively managed account will have an investment methodology that not only changes allocations into various asset classes but also changes the weightings of those allocations and also changes into something sometimes called a Total Return style of management. The point is, that Model Q™ does not function when chasing returns or chasing an allocation method. Model Q™ functions to generate a reliable Income Stream or Cash Balance. Managing for Investment Return or Managing for an Allocation Model is not a predictable management system for generating Cash Value in the Modern Financial Industry. A static allocation model or rebalancing is simply not reliable for income generation by itself according to Model Q™ requirements.

There are many different techniques of active management that you may have heard of. Some are called total return some are called equity return some are bond timing services many of them include hard-to-value assets such as currencies hedge funds and precious metals.

We are not going to talk about most of those but only emphasize what a management system really should be based on Model Q™.

Model Q™ assumes that if a client pays for management, then the management needs to be aware of the changing market conditions and work to adapt to how the market changes and not simply reallocate positions between a static or slightly static allocation model. This is usually called Active Management, and it is the only broad category of investment management that can adapt to changes in the market.

JUST SAY NO TO EVEN WORSE
Advice! Buy and Hold Doesn't Work!

The fact is, Buy and Hold is a Market Fallacy. There is not even a discussion anymore on this topic…there are decades of lawsuits that have determined that an Investment Professional or Investment Committee cannot simply make a choice and hold long-term for other people's money. That is a FACT.

Professional Advisors for the Institutional Community have an increasingly harder time justifying Buy and Hold at any level at all.

Simply put, this is amateur investing (…think Dave Ramsey) and every Institutional Trader thanks you, the average investor for being a buy-and-hold investor. Small investors are encouraged to hold steady positions for long periods of time so that professional day traders and institutional services can take full advantage of daily volatility and trade order inefficiencies.

The Financial Institutions build largely static mutual funds for the amateurs and cite long-term potential returns while stating past performance is no guarantee, etc, and absolutely take advantage of that retail mutual fund structure.

How common are the words "Buy and Hold" or to Buy a plan to own it for a Long Time or to be a "Long Term Investor" This is also referenced by some slogans such as "It's not Timing the Market, It is Time IN the Market" or "It's not a LOSS unless you REALIZE it." These statements are kinda true but really abused. The meaning of the advice is to not panic with an investment position (which if you follow Model Q™ you will already have your income covered and will know how much you can invest without risk to your lifestyle!) but that is entirely different than adapting through a bona fide investment strategy and making appropriate changes.

Let's go back briefly to the BHB Study, and think critically about having an allocation, holding it for a long time, and then, 20 or thirty years later seeing the rate of return.

Now…take a half second or less and think to yourself, is this what the Institutional, Professional marketplace does with its own money?

Of course, it isn't. Not even close.

Let's take a real-life example outside of the Financial Industry. When the route you drive to go to work every day has construction closing down the road… do you still take that same road and just wait for the crew to finish up? Even if it takes hours to get clear of the slow part?

Of course not! And yet, that is exactly what Buy and Hold ask you to do with your Investments! Meanwhile, every serious driver simply takes a side road or uses GPS to get a different route and still gets to work on time.

Model Q™ actually cannot function to generate reliable income without the ability to basically guarantee reliable income.

When Model Q™ solves for Income and Cash Balance requirements, well, we need to be 'aware' of allocations and momentum but buy and hold as a philosophy is just not even in the mix. It has no place at the table and no time is spent on Buy and Hold as a result.

Buy and Hold is a High Order Market Fallacy, and the successful litigation against Financial Professionals who get paid without ongoing recommendation changes seems to confirm the lack of confidence in Buy and Hold at every level.

This is modern financial nepotism, an old-time saying masquerading as wisdom when it has been demonstrated to not just be ineffective but even punishable by fines or lawsuits!

Model Q™ will always hire and fire for competence and will not wait out a 20-year period on a kiss and a promise (or a projection!). Buy and Hold is just not viable for all of the same reasons that a Static Allocation Plan or Selected Mutual Fund Positions are also not viable.

JUST SAY NO TO MORE BAD ADVICE!
The Fallacy of Just Start Investing and It Will Work Itself Out

The best way to describe this fallacy is when I first learned how to ski. The first instruction was how to do a snowplow, i.e., cross your skis into a wedge to slow down and how to straighten the skis to go fast. Once you are going fast, you lean into turns.

And like Magic...there you are, hitting the bunny hill. "Kinda" skiing.

Well, Skiing is a pleasure sport.
Model Q™ has to solve for Income and Cash Balance requirements for potentially decades of a client's actual LIFE. It is a touch more serious.

We cannot just put money in the market, and we cannot just have a static allocation and we cannot just wait a long enough period of time to have our goals satisfied. The tried and true advice is much better stated as "Simply Invest and be prepared for it to take some time" which is not a viable option for a professional service with a commitment to excellence.

We have to work hard to take every advantage presented, including Tax advantages! (More on that later…)

Now this "Just Invest and let it work itself out" nonsense may actually be how an individual gets started with personal savings, but let me assure you. Institutional Money Management Active Money Management and most definitely Model Q™ are highly considered and targeted Investment Methods.

We don't just put on the first two socks in the sock drawer and hope they are both black socks! To be cheeky about it and demonstrate some personality, we first make sure our socks are freshly laundered! Then assembled in matching pairs! Then time is spent in the careful selection of a pair of socks to complement both the Trouser and the Shoe as it were. We hope the difference in approach is immediately notable to the reader.

There is a direct relationship between risk and potential reward. If you want to put away money and KNOW it will always be there for you, then you are Risk Averse. Model Q™ supports this requirement in a way few other methodologies even approach.

What they don't really tell an investor in plain English is that as you get closer and closer to retirement, your ability or desire for risk may be impacted…BASED ON WHETHER OR NOT YOU HAVE YOUR RETIREMENT INCOME ACCOUNTED FOR.

Model Q™ puts this in front of EVERY conversation; we do not wait for it.

JUST SAY NO TO BROKER DEALERS!

The broker-dealer model, which combines broker and dealer functions within a single entity, has been subject to criticism and scrutiny due to several inherent inefficiencies in allowing a company to both Broker the Sale of Securities not held directly and Deal in Securities that are held directly with maximum fee models associated in each enterprise.

Pay attention because the inefficiencies in both situations lead directly back to taking cookies out of any available cookie jar at the expense of both the Investor and Associated person to the direct benefit of the Broker-Dealer and the Shareholders of the Broker-Dealer.

It is a cabal of closely held interests in the guise of operating through Self Regulating Organizations. Simply put, Broker-Dealers fight any legislation tooth and nail that will impact the profitability of billing an Investor or Associated Person while maintaining as little liability as possible. That is the Business of a Broker-Dealer. A Broker-Dealer is simply not in business to be anything other than suitable and is absolutely not paid to offer any fiduciary services!

Q Financial believes that the Broker—Dealer business model is the most susceptible to replacement from Artificial Intelligence and provides the least value to both the investing public and the Registered Representatives associated with them.

1. Conflicts of Interest: Conflicts can result in biased advice (Approved products that have to pay for access) and recommendations (Revenue Sharing agreements that may / should be fully disclosed in fine print) that may not align with the clients' best interests that are, however, suitable. The kicker behind the entire conflict of interest is that by contract, the Associated Person or Registered Representative is bound to make nearly all disclosures, the Broker—Dealer is only required to Supervise those disclosures while specific contract negotiations have little to no disclosure requirements! Any errors or omissions costs are normally placed directly at the feet of the Advisor or hidden inside a payout matrix. The Biggest Conflict of Interest that is never disclosed is that the Broker—Dealer is always right unless proven wrong or fined directly. Long before that happens, the Advisor gets suspended and the compliance officer who failed to supervise generally gets suspended as well, all while the Broker—Dealer controlling parties and officers are allowed to carry on. The way that the entire BD industry has evolved is to have a layered series of scapegoat employees and representatives! The fact of this statement is born out simply by reviewing the Daily actions press release of FINRA against Broker—Dealers and Registered Persons. Persons get suspended,

and the Broker-Dealer gets fined. The entire "I am not responsible for anything" mentality is odious in politics, just like it is in Broker-Dealers.

2. Lack of Transparency: The broker-dealer model 'may' have a (really it always does but we are trying to be tactful) lack of transparency in terms of pricing and execution. There are quite a few loopholes Broker-Dealers will exploit. Promises of 'Best Execution' that are based on contractual Trade Windows disclosed in fine print for odd lots. Omnibus trade pricing and lack of discount flow to clients is another Cookie jar frequently raided for extra cookies. Pricing disparity between settlement accounts. Trade confirmations are offered with a spread of time and price to allow Front to run legally for additional trade profits.

3. End Result: Clients aren't even billed for these cookies that are raided. Trade costs are nebulous creatures that frequently lack any accounting until the following year and then, are only disclosed in supplement form. Trade inefficiencies are commonly exploited for round lot stock purchases at discount pricing to the Broker on the open market and then passed through to the Investor as a Dealer, with Principal Markup and Individual Ticket cost on the same round lot purchase. The kicker here...if these activities are a finable offense for a Registered Representative in an IRA or ERISA account or for any Registered Investment Advisor – so how is it that a Broker-Dealer can negotiate these all day long and not even have a duty to disclose except in the broadest of terms?

I guess it is just extra cookies that Broker-Dealers can keep simply because they are broker-dealers!

4. Clients may not have access to the best available prices or may not be aware of the potential conflicts of interest affecting their trades but it should be obvious that a Broker-Dealer is not in business for the benefit of the Investor. The Broker-Dealer is in business to protect its own interests and to maintain its own client base as a source of billable expenses at the expense of the Advisors hired to service those clients.

5. Supervision is a huge problem Broker-Dealers have. Churning and overtrading in particular cause damages to investors: In the broker-dealer model, where brokers earn commissions on each transaction, there is a risk of excessive trading or churning. Brokers may be incentivized to encourage frequent trading to generate more commissions or sell sponsored offerings, even if it is not in the best interest of the client. Overtrading can result in unnecessary costs, reduced returns, and increased tax liabilities. Private Label Management programs are another prime example often found with Brand Name Broker-Dealer Firms which will highlight a Manager or Subadvisor paid to do the work by the Client while the Sponsor, a Brand Name Broker-Dealer, adds a surcharge or Wrap Fee to a private label that program. Remember, if you work with a Broker-Dealer, the BD only has to make suitable recommendations and disclose in the fine print that you may be (are being!) overcharged compared to other similar programs!

6. Limited Product Offerings: Broker-dealers may have limited product offerings, focusing on promoting and selling their proprietary products or those from certain affiliated entities. This absolutely restricts client access to a broader range of investment options or unbiased advice tailored to their specific needs. It may also create incentives for brokers to recommend in-house products, regardless of their deeper 'suitability' for clients as previously stated.

Picture this: ABC product will not be sold through a particular Broker-Dealer without first paying for a Due Diligence Fee / Product Review Fee (Pay to Play) and then the BD will frequently agree to add it to a Private Management Program lineup and surcharge an additional fee at the Investor level paid to the BD. If that is not a direct conflict of interest even if disclosed, then please consider how close it borders to a direct conflict of interest.

This practice, by the way, is NOT considered Double Dipping by the Industry Regulators. It is simply common business practice! It does, however, illustrate perfectly that, once again, the Broker-Dealer Model is not in business for the Best Interest of the Client. To find that requirement, you actually have to go outside of the Broker-Dealer model.

7. Compliance and Regulatory Challenges: The broker-dealer model is subject to extensive regulations and compliance

requirements, which create administrative burdens and increase costs. Compliance processes and obligations can be complex and time-consuming, leading to potential errors and delays in client service. Additionally, regulatory oversight may vary, and enforcement actions may not always effectively address misconduct. Again- please review the daily FINRA enforcement press releases for a clearer idea of the compliance burdens and costs that are found in the Broker-Dealer Channel. Think to yourself after a week… how many of these issues are just repeat issues that continually show up in a Broker-Dealer business model?

8. Lack of Specialization: Broker-dealers are generally more focused on facilitating transactions and executing trades rather than providing any sort of specialized investment or planning advice. As a result, clients may not receive in-depth expertise or tailored guidance in complex areas such as financial planning, tax strategies, or risk management. In fact- those services may be highly regulated by a Broker-Dealer to prevent liability to the Broker-Dealer. This is especially true for designated "Marketing" Systems and "Communications with the Public" from the Broker-Dealer side of the Financial Industry. The fact is, an Advisor can be a Dual Licensed CPA and Investment Advisor and yet not be "allowed to discuss" taxes without written permission from a Broker-Dealer- who makes no business at all in Tax planning! A Published Author and Subject Matter Expert or Court Appointed Expert Witness in Estate Planning or Tax Strategies may not be able to reference any education or background about that

Experience or Level of Training by a Broker-Dealer seeking to limit firm liability.

Let me point out yet another time, that any Broker-Dealer is not in business to operate in the Client's best interest. Specifically, and as the result of many lawsuits seeking the definition between suitable, best interest, and fiduciary duties owed to an investment client!

Numerous lawsuits notwithstanding, Broker-Dealers have made it very clear that their business model is not to a Fiduciary Standard.

Every Broker-Dealer may or may not operate according to 'Best Interests' standards over 'Suitable' standards at any given point in time and it is up to the investment client to know when and how that may affect a product sale or recommendation. The Broker-Dealer simply has to throw a disclosure to the client.

By taking this position, the Broker-Dealer can then surcharge the client, and the associated person at every level. The Broker-Dealer can up-charge required Errors and Omissions Insurance and up-charge for Representative access to required software while also embedding due diligence costs for products and up-charging clients for investment products or trade order routing at the same time.

Institutional Investors and Investment Committee are already aware of these additional and unnecessary costs and negotiate accordingly or work inhouse. Model Q™ also works best outside of the Broker-Dealer model for the same reasons, to limit unnecessary costs and problems.

UNDERSTAND:
Suitability vs Client Best Interest / Fiduciary Standards

We really only brushed up against this topic while discussing Broker-Dealers so let's do a little bit of a deeper dive into the subject matter of particular differences between Suitable recommendations, Best Interest Recommendations, and actual Fiduciary Standards!

First off for a deep dive is formal definitions:

Suitability: Appropriate match between personality, circumstance, and goals. FINRA Rule 2111 further defines this specifically as gathering information related to an investor's age, investment experience, financial situation, tax status, and other investments the customer may have... ie...a burden of basic information must be gathered to create a customer profile. There is also a requirement to act in Good Faith and the responsibility of Fair Dealing... which means "Sell a Product that Fits and doesn't Lie or misrepresent details."

Best Interest Recommendations are covered by SEC Rule 15I-1 and can be succinctly described as extending Suitability requirements to Broker-Dealers and Associated Persons to include the Types of Accounts recommended- with a particular focus on the structure of various Qualified Accounts like IRAs and ERISA Qualified accounts like 401ks or 403bs. As a side requirement, a Relationship Summary (Commonly called Form CRS) is required to be distributed to Investors which details in slightly different language than what the Industry required prior to 2019, what the various roles and responsibilities are of your Advisor and a Broker-Dealer. *Note: Best Interest recommendations are a 'compromise' sought vigorously by the Broker-Dealer community to avoid a Fiduciary Relationship with a client!*

Fiduciary Standard: The CFA institute has a great definition of a Fiduciary standard with several call outs that are worth noting. Specifically, and succinctly quoted a Fiduciary Standard is defined as "Members and Candidates must act for the benefit of their clients and place their clients' interests before their employer's or their own interests."

With the further statement that: "Currently, those who provide financial advice adhere to two standards of conduct: (1) a fiduciary standard for "advisers" who are registered with the SEC under the Investment Advisers Act of 1940; and (2) a suitability standard for brokers and others that refer to themselves as "advisory" in nature. The suitability standard of care is lower than a fiduciary duty and requires only that the broker has a reasonable basis to believe a recommended course of action is suitable for the customer based on a reasonable inquiry into the customer's investment profile.

This dual structure of care creates a number of serious problems, including:

- Brokers are able to take advantage of the goodwill and trust implied by the higher, fiduciary standard of care without making the interests of clients first preeminent.

- Those not subject to the fiduciary standard create confusion among investors, not least by calling themselves "advisors" even while not being registered as advisers; Self-interested actions by those not subject to the fiduciary standard of care undermine the goodwill and trust associated with many prudent and client-oriented advisers.

What was not covered by the CFA definition but is covered by this eBook includes all of the various efforts to upcharge (quite legally) commonly available products and tools, private label low-cost or no- cost services for a fee and layer multiple fees to both Investors and Advisors in a fashion that is not considered double dipping legally, however, seems to result in fees and transaction charges and embedded costs in nearly every ancillary capacity available.

Very quickly, and simply by looking at definitions, one can conclude a sticky situation exists and is becoming increasingly obvious to regulators and investors.

The answer at first blush seems to be that Broker-Dealers are really quite set on not being accountable to make a business based on an investor's best interest at the very least and have fought very hard to maintain that standard.

Which conversely means that a Broker-Dealer must be in business at the expense of the Best Interests of the Investor...literally, and by definition.

The distinction between the fiduciary duty of investment advisors and the client's best interest standards applicable to broker-dealers has been a subject of regulatory debate and has changed over many years. The debate has really been guided heavily by the Department of Labor and Fiduciary Guidelines for the administration of Group Retirement plans like 401ks, 403bs, 457s, and TSP plans.

Since the 1990s, lawsuits against Group plans have been increasingly successful when reasonable oversight and care for administration are lacking. This has gradually led to ever-increasing standards for Individual Retirement Accounts, however, it has not yet penetrated Individual, Joint, or Trust accounts...any of the Non-Qualified Investment accounts are still only held to basic suitability standards... and remember...this means all your cookie jars are out there on the table before you even know what is going on!

Now that we have established definitions, let's actually break down a sample encounter with a prospective investor,

Mr. X. We will run a sample encounter with Mr. X for both a Suitable Investment, and a Best Interest overlay and also with a Fiduciary Standard level of service.

Traditionally, broker-dealers were held to a suitability standard, meaning they were required to recommend investments that were suitable for their clients based on their financial situation, investment objectives, and risk tolerance when a broker-dealer was making a sale of a stock-bond or mutual fund or product.

Basic investor profile information was then strengthened to require additional burdens of fact before making a recommendation.

While the "best interest standard" under Reg BI represents an elevated 'obligation' for broker- dealers, it falls short of the fiduciary duty imposed on investment advisors by a fair measure and still rewards the sale rather than the service and in addition, the program or position that is sold has a lot of potential holes just in the very structure or not having to prove the existence of a "Good" or even "Competitive" recommendation. A 'Suitable" investment by definition can actually include an investment ranked at #100 out of 100 options by definition...and that position can be maintained indefinitely through a "Suitable" allocation model.

Buyer beware indeed.

The "Suitable" Investment further Explained:

Our Broker-Dealer for this example is "XYZ Investments." Here's how a broker from XYZ Investments will work with Mr. X:

1. Client Engagement: The broker from XYZ Investments engages with Mr. X to gather information about his investment goals, risk tolerance, and financial situation. They may conduct an initial meeting or conversation to understand the investor's needs and objectives. Know Your Customer or "KYC" information is gathered such as Photo ID.

2. Investment Recommendations: Based on the information and objectives Mr. X provides, the broker provides investment recommendations. This is typically "Growth" or "Income" or "Speculation" as an Objective, and will often ask if a client like Mr. X has ever used Mutual Funds or Insurance or Stocks or Bonds or Alternative Investments in the past and roughly for how long. The recommendations often include specific investment products such as stocks, bonds, mutual funds, or other financial instruments. The broker may indicate how they are paid but are not obligated to discuss exact commissions or benefits associated with the recommendation— this is all explained on the Form CRS which is handed to Mr. X during or before the first meeting that a recommendation is made.

3. Commissions and Compensation: In a commission-based model, the broker receives compensation through commissions

earned from the purchase or sale of investment products.
When the average investor executes a trade based on the
broker's recommendation, the firm receives a commission
from the transaction, and a portion of that commission is
typically paid to the broker as compensation. Additional
Monies may be paid to the Broker–Dealer in addition to
the "Haircut" that the Broker–Dealer Charges to the
Associated Person. Remember, this is NOT considered Double
Dipping when a Broker–Dealer gets paid on both ends, it is
considered Double Dipping when the Associated Person or
Registered Representative gets paid on both sides of the
transaction, however!

4. Execution of Trades: If the average investor agrees
with the broker's recommendations, the broker proceeds
with executing the trades on their behalf. The broker
may use the firm's trading platform or liaise with other
financial institutions to facilitate the purchase or sale
of the recommended investment products.

5. Ongoing Communication and Monitoring: The broker
maintains regular communication with the average investor
to provide updates on the investment portfolio's performance
and market conditions. They may also offer recommendations
for adjustments or rebalancing the portfolio based on market
trends or changes in the investor's circumstances. In these
cases, the Broker does get paid if a new recommendation is
followed that generates a new sale or trade.

It's worth noting that in a commission–based model, the
broker's compensation is tied to the investment products

they recommend and the transactions that occur. This is frequently abused. It is called "Churning" or "Excessive Trading" and a Broker-Dealer is supposed to Supervise an Associated Person to help prevent "Churning" but it still occurs with some regularity, especially with merely 'suitable' recommendations!

While a Broker-Dealer and Associated Person will aim to provide suitable investment advice, there are inherent conflicts of interest in their very structure *which does not need to be disclosed* at all levels of the client engagement. The Broker-Dealers approved product list frequently features override agreements or sales agreements that feature a BD-specific revenue stream that is not specifically disclosed at the client level because the requirement is for 'maybe' an Advisor-level conflict of interest disclosure and that is only for some account types subject to Best Interest standards! Brokers are absolutely incentivized to recommend products that generate higher commissions simply by having a Broker-Dealers Approved Products List to draw upon. It is, once again, buyer beware! The Form CRS will reference some pretty vanilla disclosures which are the extent of what the Industry Requires. Contact any Broker-Dealer or Registered Representative and ask to see their Form CRS.

There is no obligation for further disclosure than that Form from the Broker-Dealer or the Associated Person!

Another Example of a Suitable Investment Recommendation worded differently:

Mr. X is a 35-year-old professional with a moderate risk tolerance, a stable income, and a long-term goal of saving for retirement. After conducting a thorough analysis of Mr. X's financial circumstances, investment objectives, and risk profile, a financial professional operating under the financial suitability standard may recommend a diversified portfolio consisting of a mix of stocks, bonds, and mutual funds.

The recommendation takes into account the minimum standards of Mr. X's age, allowing him to benefit from the potential growth offered by equities over the long term. Additionally, the inclusion of bonds and mutual funds helps to balance the portfolio's risk and potentially provide stability and income. The specific asset allocation and investment products within the recommended portfolio are tailored to Mr. X's risk tolerance and investment knowledge to hopefully align with his individual circumstances.

As an example, the financial professional may consider Mr. X's preference for socially responsible investing and incorporate suitable investment options that align with his values. This recommendation reflects the financial suitability standard's objective of finding an investment solution that suits Mr. X's immediate needs and objectives.

However, it is important to note that this recommendation under the financial suitability standard may not necessarily take into account all the factors considered under the Fiduciary Best Interest Standard. For instance, the financial professional may not be required to disclose any potential conflicts of interest arising from the investment products recommended, nor would they be obliged to assess the impact of fees on Mr. X's long-term returns.

In contrast, under the fiduciary best interest standard, the recommendation may undergo a more comprehensive analysis. The financial advisor would consider a wider range of factors, such as the cost- effectiveness of the investment products, potential conflicts of interest, and the impact of fees on Mr. X's overall investment returns. This higher level of scrutiny ensures that the recommendation is not only suitable for Mr. X's immediate needs but also aligns with her long-term financial well-being and minimizes any potential conflicts that may arise.

Example of a Fiduciary Best Interest Investment Recommendation for Mr. X:

Let's continue with the hypothetical scenario of Mr. X, the 35-year-old investor with a goal of saving for retirement for an apples-to-apples comparison. Under the fiduciary best interest standard, a financial advisor would undertake a more comprehensive analysis of Mr. X's financial situation, long-term goals, risk tolerance, and other relevant factors.

Based on this thorough assessment, the advisor would provide an investment recommendation that prioritizes Mr. X's overall financial well-being and not just the sale of an Investment, suitable savings and reduced debt are frequently part of an analysis.

In this case, the financial advisor may recommend a diversified portfolio with a long-term perspective, tailored to Mr. X's risk tolerance and investment objectives. The advisor would carefully consider various investment options and factors such as historical performance, expense ratios, and potential risks associated with each investment.

Furthermore, the advisor would assess the impact of fees on Mr. X's investment returns, making an effort to recommend cost-effective investment products that minimize expenses and maximize potential gains. The Fiduciary Advisor would be transparent about any fees or commissions they earn from the recommended investments, ensuring Mr. X's full understanding of the costs involved.

Additionally, under the fiduciary best interest standard, the financial advisor would strive to mitigate any potential conflicts of interest that could compromise Mr. X's interests. Proprietary Products would have to demonstrate lower cost or better metrics to be considered. The Fiduciary would disclose any affiliations or incentives that might influence their recommendation, ensuring transparency and allowing Mr. X to make informed decisions.

Considering Mr. X's long-term retirement goal, the fiduciary advisor may suggest a combination of low-cost index funds or exchange-traded funds (ETFs) that provide broad market exposure and have historically shown consistent returns. This recommendation would align with Mr. X's financial well- being, as these investment options offer diversification, lower expenses than Mutual Funds, and long- term growth potential.

Throughout the investment process, the fiduciary advisor would maintain regular communication with Mr. X, providing updates on her portfolio performance, rebalancing recommendations, and adjustments based on any changes in her circumstances or market conditions. This ongoing relationship and duty of care exemplify the fiduciary advisor's commitment to acting in Mr. X's best interests. In stark contrast to the Broker-Dealer Model of soliciting for sales or trades, the fiduciary advisor will get paid an ongoing percentage, as the account grows, so does the Advisor's compensation. This ensures that interests are aligned and that in almost all cases, trades are prepaid out of the Management Fee charged. There is every incentive for the Fiduciary to grow Mr. X's investment!

By adhering to the fiduciary best interest standard, the financial advisor ensures that the investment recommendation is not only suitable for Mr. X's immediate needs but also considers her long-term financial goals, minimizes conflicts of interest, and maximizes the potential for her financial success.

This eBook is obviously slanted against the Broker-Dealer business model and has hopefully provided enough data and examples to support that position.

Investors truly need to be wary! Brand Name Investment and Brokerage Firms overwhelmingly tend to own the client relationship and then hire servicing advisors. These servicing advisors have production requirements, scripts to follow, and products to recommend. If the servicing advisor doesn't perform with sales goals, then they are replaced, and you get a new advisor calling you up to introduce themselves because the last servicing advisor "left the firm".

Independent Advisors have almost always pulled away from the Wirehouse or Broker-Dealer environment due to all of the inherent issues and monkey business. Independent Advisors can be Fee- Based or Fee-Only, but whether or not they own the Client Relationship is absolutely worth knowing. Commission products can be part of your portfolio in which case the advisor should leave you with a thorough understanding of when that advisor is getting paid a commission and when they are paid a fee.

Fee-Based firms tend to be solicitor firms. This means that a Fee-Based Firm or Advisor is most commonly one that manages the client relationship and finds investment products and programs that complement the client's goals. This approach is terrific because you have maintained the separation between creating and managing the Investment, and the Client Relationship. Where this runs bad is when excessive fees or internal programs are recommended that are far more expensive than widely available counterparts.

This is a huge problem that one encounters with Brand Name firms and Servicing Advisors in particular, and since a Fee-Based firm is also subject to Fiduciary Obligation and operating in a Client's Best Interest, you can see why it is important.

Indeed, the only surprise is that *it is as common as it actually still is* in the year 2023 to find uninspired and sub-par investment programs with no real track record of success and an expense load double or more of commonly available counterparts... due to the nature of the wrap program involved.

Just call up a brand name firm or a Bank owned securities department and review their managed account programs! You will probably find something like the following:

A Well-known Brand Name or Bank Owned Broker-Dealer will have, a servicing advisor to manage the client relationship that offers a group of mixed C share mutual funds (Generally No CDSC which is not-quite 'No Load'), Closed-End Funds (not publicly traded and largely static mutual funds with a sales charge that is frequently Proprietary) and Exchange-traded funds. These positions are managed once a quarter in a Wrap Account for a Fee (usually about 1% to 1.5%) and are periodically re- allocated. There is a Process involved, but it is just highly questionable whether the pricing is 'Reasonable' and if the entire program is actually in the

Client's Best Interest.

The above situation is absolutely prevalent in modern society and the only way to not be caught up in it is to take the time to do your own Prudent process. Hire a third party to make a formal written statement about the pricing of your investment program. ESPECIALLY if you are with a Brand Name, National Investment Firm, or a Bank-Owned or Bank Partnered Investment Firm!

Naturally, Q Financial cuts all of these embedded Broker-Dealer shenanigans completely out of the mix! It simply does not make any sense to have that much extra portfolio drag when solving for Income with Model Q™. Literally, a percentage in portfolio expense saved is equal to at least 1.2% extra return solving for income and cash balance!

If there is no value to a Broker-Dealer relationship that is one thing, if it costs extra money that is completely different! To Model Q™, if there is no value then it gets replaced. If it cannot perform, it gets replaced. Maybe a Broker-Dealer relationship is +/- "ok" for anything involving a required income or cash balance, but even then? Why pay percentages extra for a service that is only suitable at best and tries really, really hard to remain lackluster in every sense?

It is a clown show…simply look at the corporate headquarters and staff behind the major Broker- Dealers and bank-owned and bank-partnered firms and it should be immediately apparent how many extra cookies disappear from client portfolios and the earnings of associated persons to promote that image of success...all based on merely "suitable" transactions.

The entire industry model is basically high fructose corn syrup and fillers!

So- How do you really start to Understand the Fiduciary Process?

Familiarize yourself with the Department of Labor guide for Business Owners managing a Retirement Plan. This is a Free Resource and should be required reading for anyone and everyone in a Group Retirement plan on an Investment Committee. Fiduciary and Prudent Person Rules are most frequently tested in this space, and indeed, are sourced largely from the Department of Labor rulings when brought to State or Federal Level scrutiny.

The hallmark of a Prudent Person or Fiduciary Obligation is based upon "Process" and whether that "Process" is followed and can be proven to be definitively in the best interest of the client.

How might a process be defined as being in a client's Best Interest? When making a recommendation, is that recommendation Fair and Balanced...IE does it explain both pros and cons? How many and what type of comparables are used? What is the base-level due diligence report? Were outside Consultants or Advisors solicited for formal written opinions?

Here are some examples of, (quite frankly) sloppy Fee-Based firms that really stretch a reasonable definition of being in the client's Best Interest or acting as a Fiduciary, but you will run across them!

1) A Dual Licensed CPA and Advisory Service that Only Recommends funds from one Fund Family. I'm not even sure where to start with how obviously wrong and lazy this approach is. Run fast from ANY 'advisor' making such a representation or at least ask to see the National Ranking for the Funds being recommended and pay attention to expense loads.

2) A National Investment Firm that only recommends a Stock Portfolio. Really? I am 80 years old and have a fixed income and this is my only savings. The Wall Street Rule of Thumb says I should have about 80% of my money in Fixed Income instruments, Model Q™ says I need to have all of income tied down before I even think about Risk…and yet this firm will put 100% of your money in a Managed Stock portfolio, fully subject to market risk?

3) A Specialty Investment Service that packages together Private Investments and Notes for clients and also handles the reporting of the packaged products to the clients without third-party verification. (Well…if you didn't recognize this one, you can be forgiven because, in spite of years of whistleblowers, FINRA also didn't recognize

the Bernie Madoff Ponzi Scheme until it blew up.) So- this third example, you don't technically have to worry about, Examples #1 and #2 and others like them are still out there in great numbers.

Remember — a Fee-Based Firm is simply concerned with being paid for Advice. There are some easy rules to follow to get paid for your Investment Advice, however, the entire element of Fiduciary Obligation is a separate series of tests.

If the Goal is to be paid for Advice, and the obligation is to perform in a client's best interest with a Process — that Process needs to be pretty airtight to be legitimate. Only recommending Funds from a single Fund family is unbelievably sloppy, and to think a dually licensed CPA and Advisory Service only reviews ten or so funds out of the tens of thousands, with no concerns of pricing or strategy duplication/overlap is incredible, yet this is a real-life example of a successful and thriving practice as are each of the others cited, well... except for the late Mr. Madoff who is successful no longer in every sense.

You may find a 401k or Pension Plan that will largely recommend only one platform of Investments...but there is always the option to have a "Window" into other investments outside of the single company. Great care is taken with the Fiduciary process to support Investment Selection from only One Fund Family in these cases. Frequent Subadvisors and Third-party Supporting Research are involved. Why?

Because the companies that did not take those extra steps have been successfully litigated against for decades.

Now why should your investment be any different at all?

One of the largest Independent Advisory Firms in the USA is well known for an Only-Equities approach to Investment recommendations. This approach is more of a philosophy and not exactly a fully accepted process in the author's opinion. It would be very hard for any paid third-party consultant to state in writing that an Investor should only be in US Domestic Equity Stocks, regardless of age for the entire portfolio when the greater part of the Investment world would consider this to be Sector Investing. This 'Philosophy' is actually contrary to the essence of Diversification and the implication of Sharpe's Efficient Frontier risk modeling. It really is a sales pitch disguised as an investment service.

JUST SAY NO
to Bad Financial Advisors!

Well, we talked about Broker-Dealers and problems inherent with that entire system, but you can still find good Advisors within a BD structure. A lot of really good Advisors start at a BD, many manage to make a career out of it even though truly gifted Advisors always seem to break away from the inefficiencies of a BD system.

Well, let's take some time to examine the Bad Apples, which can be found in all parts of the financial industry, servicing clients.

To best understand a Bad Financial Advisor, let us first define a Good Financial Advisor.

A "Good" financial advisor knows Financial Products very well, offers Investment Advice on the use of those products and how they interact, and will listen to a client's needs. Honesty is usually high on the list of traits of a Good Financial Advisor...but honesty itself is hard to screen for, however, the absence of Honesty is usually a defining characteristic of a Bad or Failed Financial Advisor.

Honesty and Integrity both usually go hand in hand but are slightly different. Honesty is generally regarded as being truthful, but that is not really the entire picture, is it? One can be Truthful and wrong quite often. So, the ability to actually Recognize Truth is a required component of being successfully honest. Again…this is difficult to test for, but integrity is a bit easier to solve as a desirable trait in your advisor.

Integrity is simply doing what you said you would do. Responsibility shows when taking ownership of a failure and working to correct that failure.

This all sounds pretty simple, but anything other than these few traits of a "Good Financial Advisor" is up to personal preference. Some defining characteristics of personal preferences might be 1) Appearance 2) Right Social Circle 3) Being either a Teacher of Financial Strategy or just a Solution Service 4) Making the effort to Form a Relationship 5) Gets Good Returns Consistently 6) Calling the client when there is bad news 7) Owns their own Business and is experienced with Business Owner level situations 8) Doesn't Own their Own business and only does Investment Advice 9) Is referred to a client by a friend or Colleague 10) Goes to Church – the list goes on but personal preference potentially gets kinda far into hard to define characteristics. There are plenty of Investment firms that invest by Horoscope formally as an example, so you should have no problem finding some sort of Financial Advisor with traits you find desirable.

In summary, a 'Good Financial Advisor' is simply one who

knows the products and how to use them and will listen. A Good Financial Advisor may have desirable traits like Honesty and Integrity and be a Conscientious or Responsible individual.

Once you define what you consider a Good Financial Advisor, you will have no issue finding or qualifying a 'Bad Financial Advisor.'

So, a Bad Financial Advisor will not know financial products very well and will be either unethical or irresponsible by definition. There are some shortcuts to determining Knowledge levels as well as Ethics and Integrity, but there are failure points for each that are also worth knowing about.

Short Cut #1 – Extra Credentials. Extra Credentials in the Industry, such as a Certified Financial Planner (CFP™), Charter Life Underwriter (CLU™), or Chartered Financial Consultant (ChFC™) are good first-blush indicators of extra training. A Master of Science (MS) in Finance is also a good sign. These all indicate a greater degree of training and test-taking skill. The Downside of relying upon credentials exclusively is that these Designations are all paid-for services. Older Advisors are far more likely to have just bought the designation under relaxed standards when the Designation itself was new and soliciting for members. Frequently Advisors are grandfathered into a new designation if they only pay a fee. In short… the test requirements and knowledge requirements may be

KEVIN BRUNNER & CHRISTIAN M RAMSEY AIF®

quite subjective and vary all by themselves like within a tranche of Professionals that are all CFP™. CFP™ program requirements have changed drastically since the 1990s. In modern times, it is an excellent predictor of Advanced Training, our only observation is that one should never trust a designation all by itself without understanding the context of that designation, it is paid for!

Education, Knowledge, and the ability to think together are not necessarily the byproduct of a designation. We have all seen really dumb smart people after all!

Another downside to what can be considered the "designation chase" for a quality financial advisor with multiple designations is that very cerebral advisors often have a hard time communicating with clients and commonly suffer from what is called "Analysis Paralysis".

Analysis Paralysis can often feel evasive and dodgy – where there is not a hard answer to a direct question. This can be very unsettling or even feel shifty to investors.

Advisors in this category would be better served by being able to understand and define product relationships and communicate a methodology. Conversely, a Know-It-All Advisor is just as bad…if they KNOW the answer and frequently browbeat clients and have a very certain attitude, then why aren't they retired comfortably and independently wealthy themselves? The answer is because they just like telling people what to do, right or wrong.

Each of these types of advisors has the same character flaw expressed slightly differently. They don't like to be wrong or don't like to be challenged. Once you know the character flaw, you know what signs to be extra watchful for.

Shortcut #2 – Extra Curricular activities will show deeper character insights into your advisor. Do they Volunteer? Do they play sports or have a Hobby, do they sit on Boards? Each of these activities may show insight into Character, Ethics, and/or Self-Discipline.

The downside of this approach is that it is very easy to be misled by an Advisor who just collects activities as 'notches on the belt' and specifically mines the groups for possible clients. This is definitely a tried and true way for a Financial Advisor to meet like-minded folks and market for clients, while also supporting a cause. It is very easy, even common for sales Advisors to specifically market through extra curricular activities while searching for clients. There is no education requirement for this approach, and it is a very successful way to meet new people.

Shortcut #3 – Authors and Public Figures as Financial Advisors. This is another version of qualifying your selected advisor. Are they an Author or Public Speaker or an Educator of other Advisors? Being Published demonstrates methodology, knowledge of the Industry or Products, and the self-discipline to have either a program or a collection of words. One also has the benefit of seeing a little character and hopefully understanding the personal preferences of the Advisor in this category.

The downside of a Public Figure or Author as a Financial Advisor is that they may be stuck in a methodology or a technique and not be able to branch out of it. It is common for a Book author to disdain entire classes of assets as an example, without knowing when that asset class is actually useful. Self-help Gurus of the financial landscape have their own place and their own audience.

And yes, the irony of the previous statement is noted for our entire chapter on Market Fallacies and our critique of the Broker-Dealer model in particular. Hopefully, enough reasoning has been applied to give the reader more facts than an opinion of how those criticisms have been developed over time.

In summary, it is fair to say that there are far more good financial advisors than bad ones and that the industry is fairly good at separating the bad advisors from public purview before they do too much damage. I hope the examination of traits and pros and cons gives a reasonably balanced approach to finding your Advisor and understanding where the weaknesses of your selection process or your Advisor's style may be best monitored.

Examples of BAD ADVISORS

Let's share some examples of Bad Financial Advisors and what traits a Bad Advisor may have that might be a warning sign. If a Good Financial Advisor is Honest and has Integrity, then a Bad Financial Advisor will of course, not be quite so honest and may not have 'super strict' ethics or will rationalize themselves into dangerous activity periodically. Warning signs, the author finds, are generally ego- related, which is going to be a tough one to solve because the Financial Industry only rewards strong egos and disciplined individuals, and those that also happen to be gifted with Social Interactions.

The Role of Ego in Creating Bad Financial Advisors

When it comes to financial advisors, ego can play a significant role in determining whether they are good or bad. While a healthy level of confidence and self-assuredness can be beneficial, an inflated ego can lead to detrimental outcomes for both the advisor and their clients. Here, we will explore how ego can create a bad financial advisor and why it is essential to be aware of this trait when seeking professional financial guidance.

1. Overconfidence and Neglect of Due Diligence
An advisor with an inflated ego often believes they have all the answers and that their way is the only right way. This overconfidence can lead them to neglect thorough research and due diligence when making investment

decisions. They may rely too heavily on their instincts and ignore crucial data or market trends, exposing their clients to unnecessary risks. The author likes to call overconfident Advisors either the One-Trick Pony Financial Advisor or the Brow Beater. Frequently the Overconfidence comes from just telling clients what to do and to have a good, polished presentation. Test for this by exploring Education and asking for deeper explanations to see if the Advisor has several levels of reasoning or just repeats the same advice in a loop.

2. Lack of Accountability and Blame-Shifting

Ego-driven advisors may struggle to admit their mistakes or take responsibility for poor investment outcomes. Advisors will make mistakes and there will be loss years for nearly every investment. How an advisor admits to and deals with these occurrences will tell you a lot. Instead of acknowledging their errors, they may shift blame onto external factors or even their clients. This refusal to be accountable for their actions can lead to a breakdown of trust between the advisor and their clients, ultimately harming the client's financial well-being.

3. Chasing Status and High-Risk Strategies

Financial advisors with inflated egos often seek validation and recognition through high-risk investment strategies or by aligning themselves with prestigious clients or financial institutions. Name Dropping and Exaggerated Claims of performance returns highlight this issue. These Advisors may prioritize their reputation and the appearance of success over the actual financial security and goals of their clients. This can lead to reckless decision–making and expose clients to unnecessary risks that may not align with their risk tolerance or long–term objectives.

4. Limited Listening and Inflexibility

Ego–driven advisors tend to be less receptive to feedback or differing opinions. They may dismiss their clients' concerns or fail to listen attentively to their needs and goals. This lack of empathy and flexibility can result in a one–size–fits–all approach to financial planning, disregarding the unique circumstances and preferences of individual clients. Consequently, clients may find themselves stuck in less suitable financial strategies that do not actually align with their specific requirements. (And yes, again the Author must note the unfortunate situation of Model Q™ being portrayed as a one–shoe–fits– all idiom of investment wisdom. It is hoped that the Reader has read and understood the arguments made as to Income planning over Investment Allocation and further understands the differences between systemic and unsystematic risk and how Model Q™ was born from an understanding that grew out of formal training and years of experience.)

5. Conflict of Interest and Self–Serving Behavior

Bad financial advisors driven by ego may put their own interests above those of their clients. They may recommend investments or products that generate higher commissions or fees for themselves, rather than selecting options that are genuinely in the best interest of their clients. This conflict of interest will compromise the advisor's fiduciary duty and can lead to financial harm for the clients who rely on their expertise.

How the Government Defines Bad Financial Advisors through Legislation and Censure

It may also be helpful to look first at how the Government (both State and Federal) may define an "Illegal" Transaction… as these actions by Financial Advisors are excellent "Bad" examples and a look at the personalities may help further define warning signs.

Here are a few recent examples from the SEC website:

Nov. 9, 2023, SEC Charges Former Co-CEOs of Tech Start-Up Bitwise Industries for Falsifying Documents While Raising $70 Million From Investors.

Nov. 2, 2023, SEC Charges Royal Bank of Canada with Internal Accounting Controls Violations.

Nov. 2, 2023, SEC Charges President/CCO of Prophecy Asset Management Advisory Firm with Multi-Year Fraud.

Nov. 2, 2023, SEC Adopts Rules for the Registration and Regulation of Security-Based Swap Execution Facilities.

Nov. 1, 2023, SEC Charges Crypto Company SafeMoon and its Executive Team for Fraud and Unregistered Offering of

Crypto Securities.

Also – be sure to check out the report of Fines and Censures released by FINRA Monthly Disciplinary and Other Actions report which seems to highlight some 30 to 80 actions each month and give details as to each offense.

The report can be found here:

https://www.finra.org/rules-guidance/oversight-enforcement/finra-disciplinary-actions-online or simply visit *www.SEC.Gov* or *www. FINRA.Gov directly.*

As you can see above– the government and various regulatory bodies often find fault for process– related neglect or omission. fraudulent statements, poor accounting, a lack of compliance oversight, and multi–year fraud are the highlights from just the month of November 2023 from one entity.

In summary, it is apparent that the government defines bad financial advisors with startling regularity and for the same issues that have been identified for decades. The government has a system in place to help provide oversight for obvious issues related to you, the investing public.

Q Financial encourages you to be aware of every definition of both good and bad financial advisors!

SAY YES TO MODEL Q™:

Another Explanation of MODEL Q™

Model Q™ is an offshoot of the Wall Street Rule of Thumb or the financial Rule of 100. As previously stated, this is a rough baseline metric used for allocation between Stocks and Bonds or more stated as Growth vs Income, but Model Q™ also factors for systemic risk in a way the other idioms do not seek to address.

Allocations by themselves ARE a solid time–tested and proven management of risk tolerance. If you can diversify against a risk, then the act of diversification will work to smooth out both high and low returns for a more predictable mean result over time. This is a performance metric that is associated directly with Cash Balance and Model Q™ is all about Cash Balances!

Model Q™, however, improves upon that by directly addressing some of the fallacies with the messages of modern investing. Simple Allocation by itself is not good enough when one considers systematic risk.

Model Q™ will harvest the profits from stock market gains and keep them in a safe, principally insured account or future compounding. This is a form of portfolio rebalancing but only in appearance. Remember, the focus of Model Q™ is reliable income generation first, and then investment. Harvesting extra growth and adding to a predictable income base serves to increase income, reliable income potential, and net Cash Deliverables.

The entire model was roughly plagiarized from a 1970s EF Hutton training manual. The stock portfolios and fixed annuities that Hutton used then. This rough model seems to work better as a strategy today, using the 21st-century version of modern financial instruments than it did in the 70s and 80s, even in spite of the high-interest rates of the period.

Just like cars today are better and get better mileage, today's financial instruments and accounting are better. Remember you had to change plugs and change your battery every 2 months, now you go 10,000 miles on oil changes and have 100,000-mile warranties.

Things are the same with the financial industry. There has been a lot of growth in product and access. This all works to refine older ideas to take advantage of growth and efficiencies delivered within the Industry itself.

Some strategies just get better with time. That is exactly what happened with Model Q™, older techniques were refined and adjusted for modern times and modern tools.

The classic advice has always been to just invest in the

Stock Market itself…and that advice has been built upon for decades in an effort to tune the results to the average investor. Fine-tuning the idea of investing in the Stock Market deals with the definition of Risk and Acceptable and/or Suitable Risk. Nowadays in 2023, new products are available with stricter investor protections. new technology for trading and accounting is also available. Settlement and trading can be streamlined and grouped in ways that were not possible when Stock Certificates were delivered by postal service.

Information discovery is remarkably easy. Even for Foreign exchanges and currency movements.

Using Fixed annuities and ETF portfolios today is even more efficient than what EF Hutton's advisors used in the 1970s and 1980s. The old model EF Hutton model did not pick Stocks any better, he just didn't *sell at a loss*. Neither does Model Q™. EF Hutton's models worked BECAUSE he used annuities for Income. And Stocks for Gains.

(EF Hutton also Figured out a Systemic way to Float checks and, essentially get interest-free loans day to day, which worked for years until it was discovered and then ultimately led to significant credibility issues…but that is just an interesting side note that further argues about how the Financial Industry can work against its own best interests! It was like an Institutional Finance version of the movie "Catch Me If You Can" and ultimately resulted in a rewrite of how Daily Deposit totals were aggregated by the Treasury districts to avoid "Interest-Free Overnight US Govt Loans"!)

In the 21st century, ETF portfolios and High Quality fixed indexed annuities, work even better than the original strategy.

Model Q™- It's a simple, elegant model. And it has 2 main moving parts, market up you win, and market down- you don't lose. The average return is lower, but the actual income (Cash Balance and Net Cash Deliverables) enjoyed by the client is greater. It is a more modern and better system if, for no other reason than it's a lot easier on the stomach.

Model Q™ is so elegant, even a financial advisor can't screw it up, as long as they follow the rules!

It is now so easy to become inundated with Investment Advice that a better system is needed to really delve into the entire purpose of Investing in the first place... Model Q™ and Income planning take advantage of Tax Efficiency and multi-disciplinary techniques from Estate Planning, Business Management, and Investment Management to better address Product Selection in these interesting times.

The current marketplace of investments features a Global ability to invest in various Instruments and Millisecond trade confirmations. Here in the United States, our economy features unprecedented Government Debt Levels and Historically low-interest rates. Interest rates usually dictate Income capability, thus Model Q™ and a more modern approach to defining risk and providing for Income.

2

"Just Say No"

Capital Gains Tax Strategies

GAINS TAX

This eBook will only address the following types of taxes to some degree; Capital Gains, Depreciation Recapture, and estate tax. As previously mentioned, we are primarily concerned with Capital Gains Tax and tax-advantaged exit strategies used for appreciated assets.

So what stuff is subject to Capital Gains Tax? The answer is a lot, with a lot of carve-outs and exclusions beyond just "property" "investment property" or "business assets."

IRS Publication 544 addresses directly the "Sales and Dispositions of Assets". Essentially it states that any change in disposition such as: 1) Sale 2) Exchange 3) Property is condemned or acquired by a Government entity 4) Property is abandoned 5) Property is repossessed 6)Property is Gifted it will trigger a Taxable Gain or Loss. This is also called an adjustment to Basis in effect — although adjustments to basis can also be capital expenditures or improvements etc.

The nutshell version is roughly as follows "If it is an Asset" and "If it changes Disposition or Title"...then there is either a Taxable Event or Adjustment to Basis following that event.

Keep in mind, that you actually want Capital Gains. Capital Gains is a discounted rate of what would normally be considered Income. Income Taxes for Individuals and Entities very quickly exceed the Capital Gains Tax rate. In fact, high earners and 'Dealers' of assets do not get to (in practical effect at least) claim the Capital Gains rates on asset growth. In further point of fact, your State likely only has an Income Tax…which includes taxes on Capital Asset Growth.

The IRS is the best source to go to directly for more precise information about Taxes. Publication 544 is the best single resource for Asset Sales but details are provided through other IRS publications that go into great detail about Exchanges, Options, Transfers of Property at Death, and more.

So a deeper look into Assets is called for (but we won't go too deep!).

What is an Asset that is subject to Capital Gains Tax?

Typically an Asset subject to Gains tax is defined as any sort of Depreciable Real Property. Assets are further defined in Section 1245 which offers the following helpful description as "Personal Property including Intangible Personal Property of a Character subject to Depreciation" however Revenue Ruling 2007-37 Further Defines a Capital

Asset per section 1221 as "Property held by an Individual or Business whether or not it is connected to the Business or Trade" but in certain circumstances, Property held for a Business or Trade is not considered a Capital Asset even if subject to Depreciation.

So be forewarned that Broad Definitions of Assets subject to Capital Gains are not fully reliable!

It may be "mostly" reliable to consider an "Asset" meaning an Item subject to Capital Gains or Losses may be something that easily fits into a "Category".

This definition will include Collectibles, Antiques, Bitcoin or Digital Currency, Real Property, and certain forms of Contracts or Options having calculable or assignable value that may be Gifted or Sold. Depreciation Classes of Assets are also a good indicator of an Asset subject to Gains Tax– but again, not fully accurate.

So that is as deep as we get, and the purpose of those preceding paragraphs is to give the reader some idea of how tricky the application of a tax-advantaged strategy can be!

Back to broad terms, if you have an Asset...well, you probably have a Tax or Loss associated with that Asset if you Sell or Gift Exchange that Asset.

A great question that occasionally pops up is whether or

not Cash is an "Asset." The answer is Yes…but technically, Cash is an Asset that declines in Purchasing Power through "Target Inflation" every year…and unfortunately, you do not get any formal Tax Recognition for that Inflation-Related decline in Value (I wish we could get an offset for depreciation of purchasing power!). So…Cash is a Depreciating Asset and Cindered Property but not a formal Category of Depreciable Real Property…UNLESS you have a Collectible US Mint Coin, for example…at that point, you may choose to retain currency value or claim Collectible Value and use a Depreciable Asset class instead of Currency Value, and you can decide which category best fits your need.

All of this really just reinforces that Tax Related specifics really need careful attention by a trained professional, and Blanket Statements need to be carefully qualified!

Once again, this eBook is not supposed to be 100% accurate, but hopefully, enough care is given to the footnotes and qualifying examples to reinforce the main concepts presented and to give the reader tools to define specific situations further!

If you are like many other property owners out there, a significant portion of your net-worth is tied up in "Assets" and is not liquid Cash (Liquid Cash is not really a taxable Asset, as per our recent observation). This effect is commonly called "Being Land Rich and Cash Poor," as the original book title published in 2006 that this eBook is written from would suggest.

You can also call it "Asset Rich, Cash Poor"! The point is that you cannot spend an Asset directly. Generally speaking, one has to sell an Asset in order to gain spendable cash, but you may be able to borrow against it. In either case, there is always a trigger that will force a sale or change in disposition of an Asset at some point in time.

Property Owners, in particular, get caught in this trap all the time, when it takes a bit of effort to Sell a property and get Cash, but it is easy to refinance. Then, you may not have cash flow anymore, or a balloon payment comes due, and valuation and equity requirements to continue the loan have changed. When all of that happens, you may be forced to sell and declare mortgage over basis...and when you do that, you may have a very negative cash consequence!

Here is the problem with that entire situation: You can only leverage so much before you have a negative cash flow and are at risk of forcing a sale and then recognize all of the gains you have borrowed out as taxable income.

Business owners often invest everything in their business, meaning a future sale turns into the basis of their retirement plan.

Model Q suggests Income planning is the most important baseline Plan to account for when considering *How to Sell an*

Asset. Therefore, Model Q needs to account for the Disposition of Assets, facilitate the Exchange or Sale of Assets for Cash, and use every available Tax advantage.

So if you find that you are not following Model Q™ and solving for Income planning, or you find that your Income Needs have changed dramatically due to a Trigger event of some sort...then that is where the true value of this eBook will come directly into play!

After reading this eBook, a number of options will be available for further investigation that may provide surprising answers to the question, "What is the best way to sell this Asset to generate Income?".

You may even find that your Income Improves dramatically through Model Q™ techniques!

Considering the current Federal Capital Gains Tax rates and the punishing estate tax system, (especially for non US Citizens!) this eBook will strive to demonstrate the pros and cons of each broad Gains Tax Related Strategy currently available to property and business owners.

Understanding the basic strategies is one thing; getting an idea of what strategies best fit your goals and learning to clarify what your goals are are the real points of this eBook, and the paradigm shift of this eBook is cited on the very first page. Income planning! Model Q™!

Holding an Asset may not be the best Strategy for your Income plan...actually, it usually is not. Holding Assets is more of a growth tool for after income and cash balance needs are accounted for.

Ultimately, finding the best choice mathematically is another thing entirely and will require the use of qualified advisors from various disciplines.

So, What Exactly Are Your Choices, at least generally?

Now, there are really only five choices concerning Capital Gains Tax.

1. Pay the Tax or use Offsets.
2. Like-Kind Exchange
3. Defer the Tax
4. Gift / Charitable Gift
5. Cheat

We are really not going to fully discuss option number 5 and the technique to avoid Capital Gains by cheating or misrepresenting shifting basis, etc.

So, that leaves us with four choices to examine.

Later in this eBook are chapters concerning two different types of Like-Kind Exchanges, the 1031 Exchange and the 1042 Exchange; we even mention the 1033 Exchange.

There are several other techniques to defer the tax, and they are all based in part on Installment-like payments. Deferral Techniques include Installment Sales, Self-Canceling Installment Notes, and possibly even Private Annuities in some limited cases.

Deferral Techniques can be based on the pure concepts noted above, or they can be done through other forms like Trusts, LLPs LLCs, FLIPs, etc…. The point is that certain rules must be followed for both the structure used and all IRC 453 Rules. IRC 453 governs payments over time requirements to satisfy Capital Gains deferral using the Installment Method correctly.

A common Estate Planning technique is to use an Irrevocable Trust and some form of Installment sale to accomplish some Tax planning and Estate planning at the same time. Finally, there are many techniques involving charitable gifting that can completely avoid not only Capital Gains Tax but depreciation recapture and estate tax as well.

Note: Normal Gifting Intra Family can be a Gift of Value, a Gift of Basis, or even a Gift of Rights; each will have its own value calculation and will ultimately trigger some Adjustment to Basis somewhere but will not directly Defer or Reduce Tax liability, *but instead may spread that Tax liability across several individuals*.

In so far as estate tax is concerned, it *could* be of great importance to you. Therefore, Q Financial will deal with the basics of Estate planning and how it impacts passing wealth to your heirs in a future eBook by itself. This will cover, in a very general sense, the treatments normally prescribed for estate tax and will describe some basic powers that are relevant to most US Citizens.

Non-US Citizens have a bigger problem set in those regards and frequently lose many benefits associated with Owning Property or Depreciable Real Property in the US.

In general terms, you have just a few ways to deal with estate tax…note this doesn't really go into powers or gifting or discounting…in very broad strokes, what one can do to address estate tax is:

1. Pay an estate tax bill through Life Insurance or cash in hand.

2. Asset Freezing techniques which prevent more growth of the estate or carefully define the taxes that are projected.

3. Asset Draining Techniques involve Gifting to future generations or Charities in some form.

Fortunately, many of the techniques explained in this eBook address both Capital Gains Tax and estate tax to some degree and will serve the vast majority of US Citizens in basic knowledge of available techniques.

Depreciation Recapture is not very well explained in this eBook except to note that certain strategies remove this cost entirely and certain techniques may "sort of" defer it or may "kind of" make it go away…but depreciation recapture is best clarified by your tax advisor.

Let's take a look at a quick Chart Designed to Illustrate Solutions offered by this eBook in our Tax Planning Chapter.

Capital Gains Solutions Matrix

	Capital Gains	Estate Tax	Depreciation Recapture	Income Paid
Pay the Tax	Yes	Asset Included	Yes	Step up in Basis and Full Control of proceeds
Installment Note	May Be Tax Deferred	Asset Included	Yes	Part Gain and Part Income owed as payments recieved
Self Canceling Note	May Be Tax Deferred	Estate Drained of Value not Paid	Yes	Part Gain and Part Income owed as payments recieved
Private Annuity	Taxable	Estate Drained of Value not Paid	Yes	Ordinary Income
1031 Exchange	Tax Deferred	Asset Included	Yes	Maybe
1042 Exchange	Tax Deferred	Asset Included	Maybe	Maybe

Irrevocable Installment Trust	Tax Deferred	Asset Included	Yes	Part Gain and Part income owed as payments received
Model Q(tm) Installment Sale truts	Tax Deferred	Asset Included	Yes	Part Gain and Part income owed as payments received
CB Farmers Trust Monetized Installment	Tax Deferred	Asset Included	Yes	Lump Sum available through Loan and Gains Tax repaid over time
Grantor Trusts and Defective Grantors Trusts	May be split between heirs	Asset Removed or Included	Yes	May be part Capital Gains and part Income
Charitable Remainder Trust	None	Asset Removed	None	Ordinary Income
Charitable Lead Trust	None	Asset Reverts	None	None - Charity Receives Income
Offshore	None	Asset Included	Yes	May Be Tax Deferred, Tax free or Ordinary Income

SEE THE RESULTS OF A MODEL Q™
Income planning Asset Sale Strategy

The next few pages are the best litmus test to tell if this eBook has information of value to you! Each Page covers the end result of a Model Q™ Income planning Strategy of some flavor being deployed to produce a Lifetime Income plan.

Case Study #1: John and Betty "Smith"

JOHN AND BETTY'S CA RENTAL	EXIT STRATEGY
Bought in 1995 for $100,000	Sell Rental for $500,000
Currently Worth $500,000	Pay No Gains Tax Year of Sale
Gains Tax at Sale Estimated at $100,000	Buy $100,000 RV for Cash with Sale Proceeds
Current Net Income of $24,000 /yr	Receive Hassñe-Free income of $27,000 /yr starting One year after Sale!

John and Betty Smith are 65 years old and have a rental property that is totally paid for. This rental gives them about $1,000.00 per month in income, but John and Betty are done with Tenants and the endless repairs.

They would rather enjoy retirement and have the ability to travel and visit their kids and grandkids.

John and Betty are able to get rid of the hassle of owning their rental, are able to buy a large RV for cash, and STILL have more than double the cash flow.

This is not impossible...in fact, results of this nature are fairly typical when working with a Model Q™ Lifetime Income plan and using the right tool for the right circumstance.

Case Study #2 – Rick and Jane "Smith"

RICK AND JANE'S APARTMENTS	EXIT STRATEGY
Bought in 1999 for $1,000,000	Sell Apartments for $3,000,000
Currently Worth $3,000,000 @ 6% Cap	(Rick and Jane owed $1,250,000 after debt).
Gains Tax at Sale Estimated at $500,000	Pay Gains Tax over 20 years instead of Year of Sale.
50% of Rental income after Debt Service and Management Fees of $60,000 / yr	Income after sale is $110,000 per year for 20 years.
	$25,000 Bucket list Trip to Europe budgeted with Sale Proceeds
	$150,000 Inheritance set aside for kids immediately post sale.

Rick and Jane Smith are 65 years old and have a 50% interest in an apartment building that is going to be sold. Rick has no retirement accounts and has always worked for a commission. This apartment building is a large part of their retirement income.

Rick and Jane would like to increase their retirement income and arrange for an inheritance for their kids while paying as little tax as possible.

Rick and Jane now have no debt, no worries, a very nice trip to Europe, and almost double their income.

Maybe this sounds too good to be true, but it is 100% supported by math and applicable tax code. There is a huge difference in the income potential of $1,250,000 before Capital Gains Tax vs $750,000 after tax.

So— deploying the right Income plan really compounds the effective results! It seems like magic, but these are all strategies that the wealthy deploy to grow additional wealth.

Why wouldn't you sell a $60,000 income stream and replace it with a $110,000 Income Stream is actually the question.

Case Study #3 — Steve and Cathy "Smith"

STEVE AND CATHY'S BUILDING	EXIT STRATEGY
Bought in 2002 for $1,000,000 Currently Worth $5,000,000 @ 6% Cap Gains Tax + Recapture at Sale Estimated at $1,500,000 Current Net income after Debt Service and Management Fees of $170,000 / yr	Sell Apartments for $5,000,000 (Steve and Cathy collect $4,250,000 after debt). Pay No Gains Tax and no Depreciation Recapture. $250,000 per year is available for 5 years as a draw for income, College Tuition and purchase of Vacation Home in Costa Rica. At Age 60, Income jumps to $350,000 per year for life of both Steve and Cathy. Potential Estate Tax reduced by over $2 Million dollars.

Steve and Cathy Smith are 55 years old and have a Commercial building with multiple tenants that is the perfect investment in the perfect location and offers a lot of social benefits, but Steve and Cathy are open to receiving a higher income with less risk. Steve and Cathy have a great real estate portfolio, but this Commercial Building has been fully depreciated, and they would like to see tax-advantaged growth. If they sell any of their buildings, it would be this commercial building in spite of the name recognition and status of ownership.

Steve & Cathy now have substantially greater income for their lifetime and the additional cash on hand to pay for college expenses and a vacation home. They have reduced the amount owed the government upon their demise by a small fortune as well!

Keep in mind that what we illustrate with Steve and Cathy is only one piece and one stage of a Model Q™ Income plan that transitioned a prize investment property into a larger and more predictable income stream. This was actually a multi-layered strategy that drew upon balancing four different techniques due to the complete size of the Estate!

The results speak for themselves.

Case Study #4 — The CB Farmers Trust — Monetized Installment Sale for Buck and Susan "Smith"

BUCK AND SUSAN'S FARM	EXIT STRATEGY
Bought in 2009 for $300,000 as primary residence. Currently Worth $5,000,000 with Improvements, Livestock and equipment as Farm Debit of $2.5 Million in Equipment and Mortage Gains Tax + Recapture at Sale Estimated at $1,800,000 Current Net income after Expenses and Debt Service of $100,000 / yr	Sell "Farm" for $5.000,000 and use the CB Farmers Trust Program to defer gains tax owed but collect 95% ol sales price. Buck and Susan retire all debt post sale of $2.5 Million wilhout triggering Morigage over Basis for applicable amounts over 5800,000. Basis is retained lo reduce annual tax repayment over the next 10 years. Buck and Susan have an addilional $2.3 Million in the bank post sale which will guarantee a tax free return in US Govt Bonds of $130,000 (yr in dividend income wilhout touching principal. Buck and Susan have leveraged their tax bill to pay for itself and are earning significantly more and are paying less taxes overall. Note: Only certain Farming and Agriculture business as delined by the IRS can lake advantage of Monetizing an Installment Sale

If a normal sale was periormed, Buck and Susan would pay $2.5 Million in debt and Trigger a lax bill after exemptions of $1,000,000

Buck and Susan would have $1.5 Million post sale proceeds, which if placed in US Govt Bonds, would generate a tax free dividend Income of about $75.000 /yr without touching principal.

Buck and Susan Smith are both 50 years old and have a Micro Farm with horses and alpaca. They also have a small grow house for medical marijuana. They use the CB Farmers Trust already to defer tax on their crop as it is sold, but an injury means they need to sell their property and downsize while keeping as much income as they can during recovery.

Buck and Susan have about 50% more income and have leveraged their government tax obligation into a completely different standard of living from just paying the tax by deploying the CB Farmers Trust Monetized Installment program.

WHY NOT PAY THE TAX?

That is the whole point of this eBook in a roundabout fashion. Model Q™, after all, really puts Income planning at the front of every financial conversation but really considers the question. It is very easy to pay the tax, and you should not have any future problems except for a lack of use of the tax money you paid. You may have less income, but you will have more control.

If you 'need' the freedom to spend the post-sale proceeds, then you 'need' to pay the Gains Tax or Offset the Gains Tax with losses. Every Capital Gains Tax benefit will come with strings attached, and those strings are almost always related to access to the post-sale proceeds. If you limit that access and just enjoy Income in a prescribed fashion… then you can really get some terrific Tax Advantages and much higher performance as a result.

It seems as if Tax Planning follows Model Q™ quite closely after all! Here is how it specifically applies to the question, "Why not just pay the tax?".

If the opportunity to continue to invest large sums for even more appreciation seems like a better mathematical fit, then the whole basis of that decision should be made with the consideration of Model Q™ and having a Lifetime

Plan established before further speculation or investment.

All growth = all risk. If you haven't solved your income plan and invested speculatively when it blows up, you are just another had-it-all story, and there is no fixing that after the fact. It is absolutely an issue to get in front of!

Back to paying those taxes.

Let's talk about Offsets or what Investment Professionals call Tax Harvesting. When you Offset the Gains taxes owed with Losses realized, you adjust your basis going forward in nearly the same fashion as paying your taxes. It is a way to still get something positive from what was ultimately a poor or simply unlucky choice.

Keep in mind that the current long-term capital gains rate is between 0% to 15% or 20% for most assets held longer than 1 year as a Federal Tax instead of Income Tax. (Note the 28% effective rate for Collectibles, which usually includes Digital Currency like BitCoin for a slightly higher gains rate.)

That is still one of the lowest rates in the history of gains tax. Your state of residence may also add about 10% or so. The Point is that the combined tax on Capital Gains is probably a lot less than the effective combined tax rate you pay on any Earned Income.

That's not really so bad, is it? Capital Gains Tax IS a discount over Earned Income, and once you pay the tax owed, you have 100% control of the post-sale proceeds.

Apparently, it is bad, or you would not be reading "Just Say No" for inspiration. Just think of how much worse it used to be with Capital Gains Taxes as high as 25% to 30% Federal in years past.

That is a roundabout way of saying if the current Capital Gains Tax is bad in your opinion, chances are very high that it will only get worse as years progress. (Yet another reason to educate yourself on the tax-advantaged techniques you have available.)

The story goes something like this…

Mark and Janice were about 65 years old. They had invested in a second home in the late 1980s. When they bought their second home, they paid about $100,000. They had rented the home for several years and hoped to sell it or give it to their son; however, their son had just extended an enlistment in the army, and it did not look like he would be home or interested in the near future.

Mark recently aggravated an old back injury and was just not able to keep up the rental. Mark and Janice decide to sell the second home after talking to their neighbor, Bill, a seasoned real estate agent.

Mark and Janice were extremely pleased to find out that the second home they bought in the late 1980s was now worth $600,000. They looked forward to taking a long vacation to Europe, something they had wanted to do since they were married in 1982

The home was sold in early November 2003. Mark and Janice got their check for $565,000.00 and went to visit France, Germany, and Italy for a two-month vacation. (Due to the winter season, most of their time was spent in Italy.)

They returned home in late January 2004 and found an unwelcome surprise. A 1099 showing
$500,000 worth of taxable gain for a combined tax bill of about $125,000.00. Mark and Janice thought there was some sort of mistake because California has a 3.3% withholding on property sales. Mark and Janice had no idea this tax was due in addition to the withholding.

When I met Mark and Janice and told them all of the ways to avoid paying the tax, they were astounded.

"You mean I didn't have to write a check for $125,000!" Mark sputtered. "Why didn't anyone tell me?"

I asked them if they had consulted anyone before they sold the home. Of course, they had not; they just wanted to sell the home and be done with it as quickly as possible.

Unfortunately, the only thing I could tell Mark and Janice was that they were lucky to have only paid about 24.3% in tax and not 30% or more like it used to be, which was a small comfort.

Mark and Janice were truly upset. Hopefully, you will not make the same mistake they did.

SELL SMART BY ASKING
the Right Questions

For some reason, a professional in general (and a financial and estate planner for sure!) has to be very adept at understanding how different people communicate. This is so we can help (sometimes even lead) a client to verbalize their goals.

Make no mistake, this is a huge part of a professional's business, and it is well worth understanding to help you reach your own goals. All too often, I have seen a client amazed to realize that their motives and goals were not in line with their actions.

A holistic approach to a client interview may take a little extra time, but in my experience, it rewards the effort made tenfold.

This short chapter demonstrates how you can "wow" a financial planning or estate planning professional by clearly stating your goals after you go through the same process that is taught to those professionals for a client interview.

The story goes something like this….

One Tuesday afternoon, we received a phone call from a real estate agent who asked us to meet with a client of hers. She told us that her client was selling a piece of land and didn't want to pay the Capital Gains Tax but wasn't interested in doing a 1031 Exchange because the client was going to use the money to build a home.

The client's name was Mr. Jones. We booked an appointment for Mr. Jones to come to our office and explore the various strategies our consultants employ to help save our clients money when they sell a property.

A few days later, when Mr. Jones stopped by, almost the first words out of his mouth were, *"I don't want to pay any tax when I sell this piece of land; how can I do that?"* While this is the intended result, it is not the best question to ask, and it is definitely an issue that can only be addressed by learning more about the client's needs.

We interviewed Mr. Jones and discovered the following.

Mr. Jones is 51 and a teacher who invested in a few parcels of land as part of his retirement plan back in the mid-1980s. Being a teacher, Mr. Jones has not always had a tremendous amount of money to invest, though he has contributed to his school's retirement plan. These land parcels represent a significant portion of his current net worth and also represent a huge portion of Mr. Jones' retirement 'nest egg.' Due to the recent real estate boom, he is anxious to start utilizing the equity growth in the parcels he owns before the real estate market corrects any further.

His plan was to sell one parcel and take out a second mortgage on his home to pay for the construction of a home on the second parcel, which he then sold to build a home on his third parcel. This process will repeat until Mr. Jones has built and sold three houses, the proceeds of which will help him to retire.

Mr. Jones bought his parcels of land in California in 1987 for about $5,500.00 each. Today, each parcel is worth about $150,000.00. Mr. Jones was referred to us by his real estate agent because he was very concerned about paying the Capital Gains Tax on the sale of each land parcel, and he was not really in the position to take advantage of a 1031 Exchange since he was building new properties on land he already owned.

If the first land parcel were to sell for $150,000.00, the Capital Gains Tax would be about $35,000.00. Mr. Jones was very interested in learning ways to minimize that tax hit.

Experience has taught us that asking the right questions will produce the right answers, and the right question to ask is not, *"How do I pay as little tax as possible when I sell?"* In fact, the right question to ask when selling a property or a business is different for each seller and is the function of a process of planning more than anything else.

To sum it up in one sentence would be to say, *"What is the best way for me to sell this asset to achieve this goal?*

So, really, the right question to ask when you sell a property or a business is, "What do I need to do with this money?" followed by, "What do I want to do with this money?"

Make a quick list on paper of expenses that must be paid from the sale (an example worksheet is found on page X). For Mr. Jones, the list was very short in theory but very long in reality:

1) Use proceeds to help build a home, with an Estimated cost of $250,000.00.

Mr. Jones had over $300,000.00 of equity in his residence that would help him pay for the construction, and he could just barely afford a 2nd mortgage of about $200,000.00 for a period of about 6 months.

After gathering the facts, we were able to show Mr. Jones how he could save about $10,000.00 in Capital Gains Taxes owed from the sale of the land and have full use of the remaining $125,000.00. We were able to get enough extra money from this specialized investment paid to Mr. Jones to help him borrow the full amount of equity in his residence if he needed to during the construction.

Mr. Jones was able to sell his first completed home for

over $400,000.00 from an investment of $290,000.00 and is busy working on selling a second completed home.

Knowing the right questions to ask and finding the right people to advise you can give you a tremendous advantage when you are planning for your goals.

For example, if Mr. Jones really just wanted to save on the tax bill, he would have been smart to just do a 1031 Exchange with each parcel. However, he wanted to practice building homes so that he could personally build his own home. He also believed that he could command a higher profit from selling finished houses rather than lots, and those profits would be a nice addition to his retirement savings.

Mr. Jones had a fairly unique set of criteria to reach his goal, which is probably why he looked outside of the common technique of a 1031 Exchange to defer the tax. He knew enough to know that a 1031 Exchange would not really help him and probably would have just paid his tax if he had not learned about his options.

FINDING THE RIGHT TEAM

You may not have realized how many people work on your behalf to enact any sort of business or real estate transaction. Real Estate Agents, Title Companies, Escrow Officers, Exchange Intermediaries, tax planners, and more.

You have probably never thought about these professionals as your team. A team that you can use to help fulfill your goals.

Now, it is very fair to say that each team member usually has their own agenda and their own process to help you complete a transaction. All I can really do at this point is to show you how you can help qualify the professionals on your team and why this extra step should be done.

The story goes like this....

On a Monday morning, we received a call from a couple who saw our website and wanted to know if we could help them save taxes on an apartment building they were thinking about selling. Later that week, we met Kevin and Diane.

Kevin and Diane were in their mid-sixties and were ready to get out of property management and spend more time with their grandkids. They had owned an apartment building for several years that they purchased after selling their business in the late 1990s. The apartment building was worth over 4 million dollars, but they had purchased it for only 1.2 million. If they were to sell, their Capital Gains Tax would be over $600,000.00, and Kevin told us he just wouldn't write a check for that much to the government. Kevin further explained that they wanted to sell because the apartment building didn't pay them as much money as they would like to have during retirement.

After meeting with Kevin and Diane twice, we gave them 4 strategies to consider when they sold their building and asked them if we could meet with their CPA to discuss their options and to get the CPA's feedback. They agreed, and we were referred to Kevin's long-time fishing buddy and CPA, Barnie.

Barnie had done the books and tax filings for Kevin and Diane for over ten years and had a thriving tax practice. He was very skeptical of each strategy we offered to Kevin and Diane and refused to listen to the reasoning behind each idea or research the supporting merits of each technique unless he could charge a fee to our team and his clients.

Barnie believed that the best way for Kevin and Diane to sell their building was just to pay the tax like everyone else does and not do anything fancy unless Kevin and Diane were willing to do several thousands of dollars worth of tax planning with his company. After Barnie realized that our team would not pay a fee for his endorsement, he accused our team of trying to take advantage of an elderly couple and told us that he would never recommend his clients to work with us.

We called Kevin and Diane and told them of the disastrous meeting with Barnie and how he refused to listen to any of the ideas we offered to help them save more than half a million dollars in taxes.

When Kevin asked us why Barnie did not approve of those strategies, we told him that Barnie would not work with us unless we paid him. Kevin seemed surprised and accepted the names of a few tax advisors we had worked with in the past that might give him some insight into the techniques we proposed.

A few weeks later, we were surprised to receive another call from Kevin and Diane. They had decided to sell their building and asked us to meet with their new CPA. We asked Kevin what had happened to Barnie and found out some surprising information.

Kevin and Diane had researched some of our strategies themselves and wanted to use one of our suggestions. When Kevin asked detailed questions about the strategies of his fishing buddy Barnie, he noticed that Barnie was very evasive about providing details without being able to charge several thousand dollars to Kevin for additional tax planning.

Kevin had spoken with two of the tax advisors we had recommended to him and said that he felt something just was not quite right with how Barnie was handling his questions.

Kevin called the California Board of Accountancy and found out that although Barnie was technically not allowed to be a full CPA in the state of California.

Barnie had been a CPA in another state but had never gone to college, and California requires CPAs to have a four-year degree from an accredited college. The specific language from the California Board of Accountancy said that Barney was not allowed to sign tax returns nor be a manager of a tax planning practice… of course, Barney was signing tax returns, and his business card named him as 'Manager and Principal' of the practice.

A bit of a red flag!

Barnie had a large tax planning company that did taxes for several thousand people and had an impressive resume, but appearances were very deceiving. Barnie had been giving tax advice technically illegally while doing business in California, unbeknownst to his clients.

Further research revealed Barney had previously lived in six different states and had several lawsuits in each state in his past residence history, as well as several open lawsuits in California.

Well, the CA Board of Accountancy is ultimately responsible for policing its membership, but in this particular case, the red flags Kevin and Diane experienced led to a very surprising outcome.

Of course, Kevin and Diane's new CPA was willing to spend a little time with his new clients to tell them some of the pros and cons of each technique we illustrated.

After several meetings, we decided on a course of action that everyone understood and agreed upon, and Kevin and Diane did not have to pay for more than an hour or two of their tax advisor's time.

Kevin and Diane were very happy with the entire planning process and were pleased that they did not need to spend several thousands of dollars in tax planning illustrations just to get an idea of what their best course of action was, and now Barney is an illustration in an eBook of why you should check your professional team and qualify your advisors!

Kevin shared with us that he had learned a valuable lesson.

Kevin and Diane ended up utilizing a Trust variant similar to the Model Q™ Installment Sale Trust (although this was many years before the Model Q™ IST was crafted, there are always a great many ways to address the deferral of capital gains...some are just more expensive to set up and maintain!) to sell their apartment building. This Trust is paying Kevin and Diane over $200,000.00 per year for the rest of their life, an amount almost double what they received from owning that apartment building in the first place.

See Page 119 for the results of a properly implemented Model Q™ Income plan using available Tax Advantages to full effect!

Unfortunately, there are many dishonest businesspeople like our 'hypothetical' non-CPA (emphasis added) in the world. They can, of course, be from any profession, so always check the background of any professional you are thinking of hiring to make sure that they are qualified to give advice. Listen to the professionals' story and look for supporting documentation...practice due diligence yourself! Sometimes, a black mark on a professional's license history is actually a selling point when you learn the whole story. Learning the truth may reveal very desirable professional characteristics!

Just make sure to have a process to check the background of your professional team and see how they address any concerns you may have about their history. Keep in mind that there are many Bad Investors who also seek to take advantage of Professionals, so attempt to be as fair and balanced as possible and absolutely perform your own due diligence!

Finding the right professional to give advice can be tough. With our example, we see how to help avoid certain types of fraud or at least hedge the expense of a transaction that might be worth several hundreds of thousands of dollars to do correctly.

The next story takes the concept a little further, and it is based on how to manage your team of professionals once you have found them. Every professional has an opinion of how any given transaction should be done, and it is often difficult to listen to all sides of a discussion to determine the best solution.

You should be prepared to find out how each suggestion best suits your goal, and you should also be aware that each profession has its place and its specialty. Learning to watch the areas where a suggestion from one professional 'bleeds' into the jurisdiction of another professional is extremely difficult because specialized advice frequently combines a high topography understanding of multiple disciplines.

Stick to the basics! A financial planner cannot buy or sell a building for you, and a CPA cannot sell stocks or mutual funds or make a living from managing clients' assets. An attorney cannot give tax advice (unless a tax attorney!), and your real estate agent should not draft specialized purchase agreements for a fee nor comment on the adequacy of the terms of a contract for your needs.

The common test for Professionals is to operate within the bounds of advice, that is, whether the "recommendation" is incidental to their practice. Information is one thing, Advice is quite another thing…and charging for that Advice is the final test. Professionals talking to each other are far different than Professionals talking to Clients…so bring them together. If there is a specialized technique, listen to how the Professionals work around issues related to their field regarding the proposed technique.

Finally, a note on conflict of interest. I am absolutely positive that 99% of professionals out there are doing their personal best to offer guidance. The only problems to be aware of are those of human nature. It is very natural to develop a routine, and it is very hard to continually challenge yourself to grow and adapt when you are comfortable.

Professionals are the same as everyone else in that respect, so finding a team that is willing to contribute and research on your behalf is important. Each and every professional you hire is working for YOU, and that thought should be foremost in your mind.

UNDERSTANDING THE DIFFERENCES
between Opinions,Advice, and Formal
Recommendations!

Be aware of human nature when dealing with your team. A large portion of that is understanding how a professional gets paid to provide you with a service and what sort of liabilities that professional retains for the work performed. Opinions or Qualified Opinions can be freely offered. Advice needs to be specific to the client's situation and generally requires time spent understanding a client's situation. It usually involves a written statement and even a charge for time spent.

Everyone always tries to shortcut Advice and try to work on "Opinion" or "Qualified Opinion." ...This is the 'Ask Your Friend' or 'Mention to a Professional' version of due diligence, which is chock full of good intentions and bad results!

So, there are actually quite a few issues with that juvenile and lazy sort of approach to due diligence. Let's use some overt examples to really capture how 'Opinions' differ from 'Advice.'

1) Your neighbor is a white-collar professional who

owns a car. You tell your neighbor that your car won't start. Your neighbor says, "Did you check your Battery." Your neighbor is not a mechanic and has no idea how to test to rule out a great many issues that could contribute to a car not starting. Why waste your time or your neighbor's time? This is an Opinion and reflects conversation rather than any meaningful exchange of anything other than polite social etiquette.

2) Your neighbor is a white-collar professional who owns a classic car, or even several classic cars, and you frequently see that neighbor working on cars on weekends. You tell your neighbor that your car won't start. Your neighbor comes over, looks at the car, checks a few things, and says, "It could be ground, it could be your switch, or it could be a sensor." Since your neighbor is still not a mechanic, they do not know or cannot perform every test to isolate the issue contributing to your car not starting. This may be a qualified opinion that rules out a bunch of stuff, but it still isn't exact, and it won't hold up to any formal inquiry. This situation kind of feels like something meaningful happened, but it is really still a waste of time. Your neighbor is simply handy with cars, and if your situation is a simple one, maybe you have a quick fix. More often than not, however, more time is lost.

3) Your neighbor is a mechanic with a full-service shop that specializes in your brand of car. You tell your neighbor that your car won't start. Your neighbor

says, "Make an Appointment, and we will get it fixed." After a variety of paid tests with a qualified mechanic, you find that a piece of gravel had been lodged in an actuator, and it was causing the Neutral Safety Switch to not engage fully when your car was in Park. Your issue was not even close to being correct from Mr. Opinion or Mr. Qualified Opinion, and a lot of time and energy was wasted without correct knowledge of tests to rule out all issues affecting your car. This is a certain result, and yes, you almost always have to pay for all of the years of experience, education, and training behind the process that fixes your car rather than guesses at causes!

Don't be lazy – seek professional advice from specialists. Expect to pay for actual relevant Advice. This is exactly why a general practitioner Doctor will recommend a Specialist or why a Plumber doesn't do electrical work. An artist who paints lighthouses does not know how to build or repair a Lighthouse!

The ONLY test for "Advice" worth having is whether the Professional will commit the advice to writing, potentially for a Peer Review.

An explanation of relatively common compensation arrangements is after this next story. It is definitely something to consider when affecting a large transaction and should be important even in everyday life.

The story goes like this….

One day, we received an email from Joel asking if we could explain the Model Q™ Installment Sale Trust strategy we discussed he had heard about. We called Joel the next morning to learn more about his situation and to offer a Pro Forma report based on his answers to a Questionnaire about his specific situation.

Joel's father was thinking about selling his real estate portfolio and had asked Joel to help him research his options. We told Joel that he had called the right team of advisors and promptly set up a meeting with Joel, his father, Martin, and their attorney.

Martin had over 50 rental properties and several commercial buildings he wanted to sell, but he wanted to make sure of several things when he sold all of that real estate. Joel was Martin's only son, and Joel's Mother had died over 10 years ago. Martin had since remarried, but neither Martin nor his second wife trusted the wife's extended family. Martin wanted to be sure that his estate was passed to the future generations according to his wishes and in an incontestable fashion.

Martin's attorney was a very sharp individual who proposed to draft about six different irrevocable trusts to create a formal estate plan for Martin's estate, which was valued at over 30 million dollars. Due to the complexity of this estate, Martin's attorney would have to act as the trustee and would, therefore, have to charge a formidable fee for as long as he acted in that fashion.

Martin was a shrewd businessman and was always on the lookout for new ideas and ways to save money. When Joel had told him of some of our revocable trust techniques, he was very curious to learn more. Personally, I also think Martin wanted to see how his attorney reacted to our ideas since there was a six-figure retainer at stake for the attorney's law firm to manage his 30-million-dollar estate.

We told Martin and his attorney how each of our strategies worked and how they would address his concerns. Joel took pages of notes while the attorney did his best to demonstrate how his plan would also accomplish those goals.

What it boiled down to was our strategy would save tens of thousands of dollars in legal fees to accomplish everything Martin considered important and could be managed by a non-specialized Trustee who would not charge such a huge retainer fee for highly specialized service. The pros and cons were examined, and Martins's attorney had a very viable solution that was finely tuned; it would just require more ongoing costs for largely the same result.

What is very interesting about this story is how good the attorney was. After he saw Martin gravitating to our proposal, he switched gears and offered to manage this kind of revocable trust for Martin. Martin and Joel told us that their attorney claimed he could manage the trust and arrange to have the trust assets managed as well. Then, Martin wouldn't need to hire our team of advisors and could continue to work with their law firm.

It didn't take much to persuade Martin and Joel that attorneys specialize in laws, CPAs specialize in taxes, and Investment Advisors and Estate Planners specialize in managing Trust assets.

When you get too much bleeding between disciplines, the checks and balances of non-related business professionals working together disappear. It is always a judgment call, but in this case, it became apparent that Martin's attorney was really interested in managing all of the Assets held in multiple specialized irrevocable trusts. After that option evaporated, Martin's attorney became very interested in managing all of the Assets held in a single business purpose revocable trust.

The Model Q™ approach is to involve as many points of view and as many team members as possible on each project. This is true for helping someone roll over a 401k plan, start an IRA or SEP IRA, get insurance, or start a financial plan. It is especially necessary for Trusts.

Be wary of Attorneys and CPAs who give investment advice or manage investment assets of any sort. Though it might seem easier or more comfortable, the fact is that you wouldn't go to your family doctor for a toothache, and you wouldn't go to a dentist if you broke your leg. In this kind of situation, there is always a primary business and a secondary business, but it does allow for specialized understanding at a deeper level on occasion with the right kind of personality. Dealing with a qualified specialist with expertise is crucial, and knowing how to assemble a team of specialists to work on your behalf is very valuable knowledge.

After Martin's trust was established, we understood why he selected our team as the investment managers of his multi-million dollar trust. Martin commented that the most important skill for a business owner was knowing how to assemble a team to work together and that a business owner never stops managing his advisors. Martin personally agreed that lawyers and attorneys are there to make sure activities are legal but often end up killing more opportunities than creating opportunities. Lawyers generally have very little true experience with investments and the day-to-day activities that managing investments requires.

It is simply a different area of professional practice!

As you assemble your team of professional resources, be sure to assign each one a duty. This will help you manage your team according to your goals.

For Martin's example, he had an attorney who was to make sure that the sale of his many properties was legal and that the assets were to be held in such a way as to minimize taxation legally on a variety of levels.

KEVIN BRUNNER & CHRISTIAN M RAMSEY AIF®

Martin's CPA had the duty to provide relevant tax information and be able to understand any strategy that was ultimately implemented. Furthermore, Martin's CPA had to be aware of changes in tax law that might impact the Trust.

Until Martin met our team, his Attorney was filling the niche of working with the assets remaining from the sale of his properties that normally would be assigned to an experienced investment advisor or financial planner.

For instance, with 1031 Exchanges, you may assign a real estate agent to find an exchangeable property or limit yourself to a niche Commercial Real Estate agent for a specific type of Exchange property.

The point is to spend time finding the best people you can and hire them to do a certain job or to prepare for a certain contingency.

Be sure to ask each Professional on your team to describe how they are compensated and be sure to understand for yourself where the 'carrot and the stick' lie with each of your team members. This will do the best to help you overcome some of the human factors of negotiating a transaction.

Professionals who work for an hourly fee usually have an incentive to delay providing a solid solution. Some will try to extol the virtues of a myriad of solutions designed to help guide your decision. This eBook should assist you greatly in organizing your thoughts and activities to minimize the amount of capital spent on the strategies illustrated.

After all, if you know what you want and you know how to ask for it, it follows that the product or service should be much easier to shop for, right?

A great strategy for working with a professional that charges an hourly fee or retainer is to pay them for their time to understand a situation and then to pay for their professional statement on the matter in one paragraph to explain that situation in their own words in the form of a written statement on company letterhead.

Another strategy that works with professionals is an agreed–upon price for a service performed. I tell the professional that I am trying out their service and that I will pass their finished work to another professional to get their opinion as well. Now, if you say you are going to do this, you need to do it, but the result is that 'your process' for choosing a particular partner or service will be documented in writing, and you will have at least two opinions.

Now for commission sales, such as real estate agents, business brokers, and investment advisors. Understand how that commission is paid and try to infer the incentives.

KEVIN BRUNNER & CHRISTIAN M RAMSEY AIF®

A real estate agent may get a 6% commission to sell your property. Usually, that is split up with a listing agent so that each agent receives 3%. Then, those agents usually have to pay a broker part of their commission as well. Now, if you have a property valued at $500,000, six percent would be over $25,000 that you are paying to real estate agents. If you have a listing agent and a buyer's agent, then each agent stands to make a fraction of $12,000 to affect the sale. Each real estate agent knows exactly what the deal will pay them, and each has an incentive to make the sale on your behalf as quickly as possible. This is a good thing, right?

What is the incentive to get you, the seller, the highest price for your property? To get you an extra $10,000 above your ask price would only pay a real estate agent a few hundred dollars. If you weigh the few hundred dollars against the bulk of the commission payment for a faster deal at a lower price, then you will understand your real estate agent's incentives a little better. In terms of liability, if you have ever read a current purchase agreement for a property, the real estate agent has little to no liability for the transaction. Fortunately, the prospect of getting a referral usually keeps a real estate agent on best behavior.

For a financial advisor recommending a Tenants in Common or DST project for a commission or managing assets for a fee, the incentives are also important to note, as well as all of the fallacies previously discussed with unnecessary middle expenses in certain broad categories of Investment Professionals. The commission paid for a product must be at least partially disclosed by a financial professional where the incentive is to sell a merely suitable product.

Advisors that manage assets for a yearly fee have to disclose that fee, and they usually have to keep a client for a longer period of time to equal what a commission sale might have paid them, but then again, those Advisors have recurring revenue that, given enough time, costs more than a commissioned sale. This means that you will either have overweight to service or to cost considerations when selecting an Advisor.

Business Brokers tend to charge a commission of 10% to assist in the sale of a business, and often, they will only work with businesses that have a value greater than 1 million dollars. This is partially due to the time and effort it takes to sell a business, but it also is due to liability concerns when representing a buyer or a seller that can leave a business broker liable for years after a sale occurs, and often for a great deal of money.

Communication with your team of professionals is extremely important. It is the essence of this eBook for a reader to be aware of many professional disciplines and how each discipline can play a role in the sale of a highly appreciated asset. The intended result is a higher level of education for the reader and the ability to communicate more effectively.

Still, etiquette is equally important to keep in mind. One of the most frustrating aspects of being a professional is working on behalf of a client and then not being paid for the time and specialized skills that were used.

As the saying goes, "What comes around, goes around." So this next story is about John.

John was a real estate professional himself, with over 25 years of experience and a very successful business. I met John at a presentation about how to sell property and not pay Capital Gains Tax, and he was very interested in one of the strategies that was illustrated.

John was 63 years old, and his wife was 62. Like many professionals and their spouses, John's wife knew little to nothing about how real estate worked. That was the primary reason why John was interested in exchanging one or two of his real estate positions for a Model ™ lifetime Income plan payable to both him and his wife for as long as they were both alive, regardless of what the Real Estate Portfolio did.

Now, there are only a handful of ways to accomplish this in a tax-advantaged fashion, and John's biggest problem was that the Capital Gains Tax due on each of these real estate positions was well over eight hundred thousand dollars.

Obviously, there was a lot of incentive to avoid paying the tax bill.

It took a lot of meetings and time to prepare his trust with his attorney and answer his questions. There was even a meeting with John's current financial advisor, who had never heard of these techniques and was not at all familiar with them. (Well, he was just a stock broker and did not get paid to do anything other than broker stocks, so that is what he did!)

One of John's concerns was to not pay a ton of money to establish the trust, and he negotiated a reduction in the usual fee by saying that many of his real estate clients might be interested in using the Model Q™ Installment Sale Trust as well.

The properties were sold, and the tax bill John was concerned about was deferred. After the deal was finished and the trust assets were ready to be invested, John disappeared and quit returning calls to our team.

Since the fee for service had been formally negotiated and reduced on terms, and the work was completed, obviously, there was a breach of contract as soon as it was John's turn to perform as agreed. The contract with John as to expectations was very clear, but John did the equivalent of a professional dine-and-dash.

After several months passed, I finally caught John on the phone. He was very embarrassed and sorry that he broke his contract but offered no explanation. Well, apparently, John had some difficult personal business to attend to and decided to break his word and void his contract. Remember the chapter about Professional Integrity? John burned a lot of bridges (not just with our group) and was very quickly ostracized by the professional community.

Prudent decisions about hiring your professional notwithstanding, John did not communicate his decision to break the contract for several months and left a lot of folks hanging through his lack of responsibility and lack of character, and now he is an example of what not to do in an eBook.

When you work with a professional, no matter what area of expertise, try to be as honest and ethical as possible. I would think most professionals would reward you with extremely high levels of service because that is the kind of client each of us wishes to be affiliated with.

They say that "Birds of a Feather Flock together." If you wish to work with honest and capable professionals, then you should be honest and open as well.

MAJOR DEAL BREAKERS FOR
Tax Advantages

All tax advantages will have a list of qualifying criteria that will allow or disallow a tax advantage for a transaction. While it is absolutely everyone's right to the best and most preferential tax treatment, there is a red line that is frequently crossed. A Moral Hazard is where taxpayers or professionals seem to 'makeup,' falsify, or 'layer' into effect a series of advantages (step transactions) solely for Tax effect rather than for legitimate purposes.

This is a hard topic to delve into because, well, of course, everyone wants a tax advantage, and, of course, one can structure a business or investment to the best effect.

Let's show some examples of folks taking advantage of or abusing the system to best demonstrate what to watch out for.

1. The Marriage on Paper. Being married affords a significant Capital Gains Tax advantage for the sale of a personal residence as well as for certain rights and taxes afforded to a US Citizen that are not

afforded to a Non-Citizen. While it is 100% legal to get Married just for a reduction in Capital Gains Tax or a favorable Tax bracket in a given year, this is not indicative of good character and, in the author's opinion, represents a significant risk that a Client abusing this system will also abuse the Advisor Client relationship.

2. Assets shifting within a Family — this is best explained by the "Mob Family Asset Shifting Techniques" shown in older films where the Mob Boss holds title to assets through direct and extended family and exerts direct influence over both the asset and family. Formally, this is referred to as Related Party transactions and Basis Shifting and is so thoroughly attended to in the modern day that the definitions can be publicly found with minimal effort.

3. Not Reporting / Falsifying data. This topic covers understandable data and filing mistakes that may be part of intentional misrepresentation. Overtly, it can include keeping side books or off-the- record corporate documents. It can also include "Selling" either an Asset or a Right and taking too much of a Discount on Value or even not completing the Sale (holding paperwork at the ready). The topic also includes misuse vs. proper use of Trusts or Foreign-held Assets to obscure ownership or for asset protection and not reporting those assets or income transparently. It also includes holding undue influence or control over a

financial decision-maker.

Here is an overview of what to watch out for, but for direct definitions, it is recommended simply to take a little time on the IRS.gov website and reference each pertinent publication for the Tax Advantage you are qualifying for. Most Publications related to Assets and Capital Gains are covered in this eBook.

The basics of these 'catch' provisions will help you to determine if there will be problems with a strategy you plan on using before you even start and will also help you qualify the knowledge level of the professionals you are working with.

HOW THE IRS DETERMINES ABUSIVE
Tax Shelters and Disallowed Transactions

Every strategy addressed in this eBook is a potentially a 'Tax Shelter,' and here is a quick and dirty list of what causes the strategies to fail on a transactional basis even if the strategy has been properly formed and registered and passes all tests of structure when initially deployed.

- Duplicate or Listed Transaction – basically taking the same exclusion more than once. (1) *https://www.irs.gov/businesses/corporations/listed-transactions*

- Abusive Loss Transactions – this covers aggressive structuring of Losses to offset Gains. Certain types of Losses need to be accounted for formally on different IRS forms. (2) *https://www.irs.gov/businesses/disclosure-of-loss-reportable-transactions*

- Transactions of Interests – This is a special carve out where the IRS has formally identified high-risk transactions that include Successor Member Interests for Indirect Ownership and *assignment of Rights for Charitable Gifting benefits, Creating a Grantor Trust and then Closing the Grantor Trust for a Transaction and then re-opening a new Grantor Trust for additional benefits,*

Sale of Interests in a Charitable Trust, Basket Contracts that may attempt to convert Short Term Gains into Long Term gains by contract and finally Micro-Captive Insurance (emphasis added) where agreements are structured to resemble insurance contracts *https://www.irs.gov/businesses/corporations/transactions-of-interest*

• Confidential Tax Structures – If a tax strategy is offered to an individual or entity under confidential terms or a fee is dependent upon the realization of a tax benefit or refund, it could be a prohibited reportable transaction.

Keep in mind the previous examples are all *correctly structured Entities or Strategies* (emphasis added again) but fail on a transactional basis and not a formation basis. We don't want to get too far into the weeds with definitions, but we do want to give a high-topography review of known issues where a good strategy will still fail if the rules are not followed.

It is every taxpayer's right to find the best legal tax advantage. Taxes and tax laws are not really fun or easy for the average person; that is why there are specialists and professionals. Tax Law and Tax Codes have a surprising amount of gray area where interpretation can be aggressive or very, very conservative. Tax advisors may just use software! It is the author's opinion that a good tax advisor will understand the IRS's current intent and interpretation of allowable deductions or transactions and will explain those to a client to allow the client to choose. All that being said, we still want you to know some of the limits of legal Tax Advantages and where aggressive application of Tax Law or Contractual assignments might sound good but actually fall into Prohibited Transactions.

Ultimately, it is the Taxpayer who is responsible for a failed transaction, which is why you need to know that even if your structure is sound, the wrong choice in management or accounting can still void the tax advantage!

3

"Just Say No"

Case Studies Of Capital Gains Tax Strategies

THE INSTALLMENT NOTE

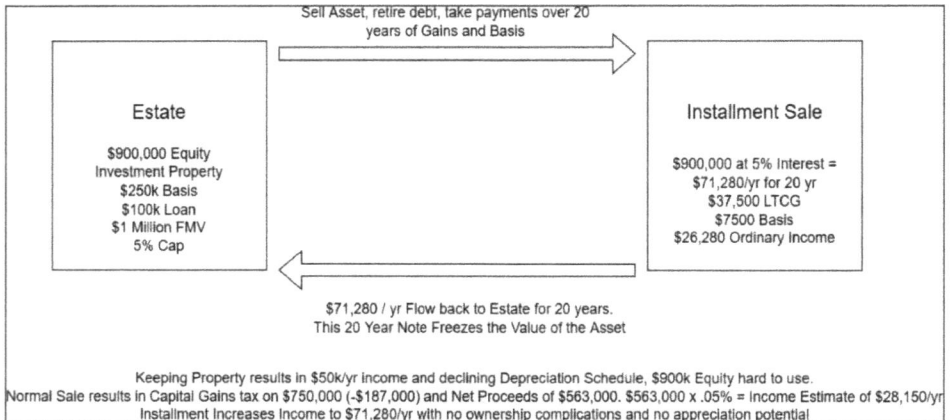

Sell Asset, retire debt, take payments over 20 years of Gains and Basis

Estate

$900,000 Equity
Investment Property
$250k Basis
$100k Loan
$1 Million FMV
5% Cap

Installment Sale

$900,000 at 5% Interest =
$71,280/yr for 20 yr
$37,500 LTCG
$7500 Basis
$26,280 Ordinary Income

$71,280 / yr Flow back to Estate for 20 years.
This 20 Year Note Freezes the Value of the Asset

Keeping Property results in $50k/yr income and declining Depreciation Schedule, $900k Equity hard to use. Normal Sale results in Capital Gains tax on $750,000 (-$187,000) and Net Proceeds of $563,000. $563,000 x .05% = Income Estimate of $28,150/yr Installment Increases Income to $71,280/yr with no ownership complications and no appreciation potential

Installment notes are one of the myriad "contractual" techniques used to sell a property or a business. However, they also allow for a deferral of Capital Gains Tax when used within IRS Guidelines for the Installment Method treatment for Capital Gains deferral. To a financial and estate planner, an Installment Note is also an estate-freezing technique.

If you have ever heard the terms "carrying the paper," "carrying the note," or "owner financed," then you may have been exposed to an installment sale instead of a simple loan or note.

153

Just to get slightly into the weeds, there is a minor difference between the terms Installment Note and Installment Sale as used by this eBook. An Installment Note is simply a Promise to Pay in one or more payments. An Installment Sale that qualifies for the Installment Method for gain reporting, however, is crafted with regard to IRS guidelines for tax advantages and is a touch more formal

For the purpose of Capital Gains Tax treatment using the Installment Method (which has restrictions on the structure of an Installment Note for allowable tax advantages), the government does not require the full Capital Gains Tax to be paid on the sale of an appreciated asset if the full amount of payment has not been received. Instead, a portion of each payment is taxed as capital gains. Another way to think about a correctly structured Installment Sale is that the tax is due as you receive your money instead of all upfront.

In any Installment Note or Sale, you are essentially becoming a lender, so the terms of the contract are especially important. Items like forfeiture clauses, security deposits (or down payments), and contract termination process need to be carefully considered and often require the services of a qualified attorney.

There are several different forms of Installment Sales that can be crafted for different Terms. This eBook will illustrate three of the more common types: a standard Installment Sale, a Self-Canceling Note, and a Private

Annuity Contract.

As far as estate freezing is concerned, an Installment Sale will serve to "lock in" the present value of an asset to protect against future growth. A potential downside is that when a seller dies, and more installment payments are due, the remaining payments can be subject to estate tax. This is called IRD or Income in Respect to a Decedent.

A standard Installment Note usually looks very similar to a mortgage note. It says something to the effect of "I will sell you this property in exchange for a series of payments over this period of time." The amount of the payment, the interest you charge the buyer, and the terms of the payments are indicated in the installment note or contract.

If your Installment Note qualifies for the Installment Method for gains tax deferral, as you receive each payment from the buyer, a portion is taxed as capital gains, and a portion is taxed as income if the Installment Sale has been correctly structured

Installment Sales have a few downsides, the biggest of which is that depreciation recapture costs are due at the time of sale and cannot be deferred. If a property has been highly depreciated, a simple Installment Sale may not make sense as a selling technique. Another problem with Installment Sales is that if the payments stop and you must reclaim the property, you might be in for a long wait as the legal process to reclaim your assets goes through the motions. When you do reclaim the property, there is also a risk that the property has been damaged and would require time and more cash before another sale can be affected.

It has been the author's experience that Installment Sales are most frequently used by very experienced real estate investors or for inter-family sales. Installment Sales are also commonly used for raw land where there has been no depreciation taken and little risk of damage to the asset. Installment Sales also get a lot of use in a variety of Trusts.

Let's take a look at a sample scenario of an Installment Sale, but remember to seek the advice of a qualified attorney before fully exploring this technique.

Erik is 65 years old and wishes to sell some land he has been sitting on for about 30 years. He inherited this land from his parents and never got around to doing anything with it. Now that he is getting up there in age, he figures he might as well look at how to sell it. Erik has never been married and has no brothers or sisters. For the past 10 years, a cattle rancher has paid him $1,000.00 a month for grazing rights on the land. Erik is thinking about selling the land to get a new truck and maybe build a nice house.

The land is about 45 acres and is located next to a cattle ranch. It is fairly close to a small town. Erik asks a few friends about selling the land and is directed to a local real estate agent, Don, who has done some work on land deals in the past. Erik also talks to his CPA, Rita, and discusses taxation.

Erik inherited the land when it was worth about $25,000.00. Now, the value is about $2 million dollars, according to his real estate agent, Don. Rita tells him his Capital Gains Tax will be about $500,000.00.

Erik doesn't need that much money and thinks it might be nicer to just "carry the note" and get some extra pocket money each month. Rita sends Erik to Jonah, a real estate attorney, to discuss his options for setting up an Installment Sale.

Jonah is particularly keen on real estate transactions and helps Erik discover that the land can be subdivided into 5-acre parcels and can be rezoned for residential use or kept for its present use as agricultural.

Erik can now decide to sell the land as one big chunk and make an installment sale or subdivide the land into nine 5-acre parcels and sell the parcels every once in a while.

Erik talks to Don and just wants to make things simple. Don suggests making a single sale but going ahead and dividing the parcels up prior to making the sale.

Erik drafts his Installment Sale agreement with Jonah's help and decides to take 20% down and offer generous terms of owner financing. He decides on charging a 6% interest rate and setting the payments up for 25 years. This means Erik will get monthly checks until he is 90 years of age.

The cattle rancher ends up buying the entire acreage from Erik and immediately using Don to sell three of the nine 5-acre parcels (the ones closest to town) to cover his out-of-pocket down payment. As far as the cattle rancher is concerned, he now owns the best grazing acreage that he was previously renting, and the interest rate Erik offered was much lower than a bank would have offered.

Erik now has enough money to buy his truck and start building his new house from the down payment. Instead of getting $1,000.00 a month from the rancher, he is now getting about $10,500.00 a month (and fresh steaks from a bonus cow a year as a perk.). If the rancher defaults on the payments, Erik reclaims the remaining six parcels. This is another way of saying the rancher couldn't sell more than three parcels until Erik has been paid in full.

Erik's Installment Sale:

	NORMAL SALE	INSTALLMENT SALE	PRO/CON
Sale Price	$2 Million	$2 Million	
Depreciation Recaptured?	None (Land is not Depreciable)	None (Land is not Depreciable)	
Amount Erik Receives from Sale	$1.5 Million	$400,000.00 Lump Sum and approximately $10,416.00 per month for 25 years	Only about $100,000.00 was paid for taxes from the lump payment. A large portion of each monthly payment will be Capital Gains Taxable.
How does it affect the Estate?	$1.5 Million is in Erik's Estate and can be used for anything.	The total sum of all payments the rancher makes to Erik is $3,524,800.00.	When Erik dies, whatever has not been paid is possibly subject to estate tax. This is Income in Respect to Decedent. There is, however, no concern for the future growth of the asset as the price is now fixed.

The bottom line is that an Installment sale is an easy transaction to perform, and it does lessen the impact of paying Capital Gains Tax to a degree; however, the benefit for estate tax consideration is relatively small. Erik is certainly able to purchase life insurance to help control a definite estate tax impact if that is important to him. Normally, an Installment sale is used for Intra-Family sales or for the sale of land. Since this technique does not address depreciation recapture costs and due to possible loss of value from forfeiture, an installment sale is rarely used for investment, income, or commercial properties unless it is through a trust or special purpose LLC.

SELF-CANCELING NOTES AND PRIVATE ANNUITY CONTRACTS

Self-Canceling Installment Notes (SCINs) and Private Annuity Contracts* are forms of Installment sales that are almost always used for inter-family sales, primarily as an estate freezing technique to help protect a family from estate taxes. However, like a correctly structured Installment Sale, these alternative tools may also serve to defer Capital Gains Taxes until payments are received by the seller. This means that Capital Gains can be paid over time and then passed as an inheritance as an adjustment to the basis upon the seller's death by contract.

A SCIN looks exactly like an Installment Sale except for a critical addition. It would look like this: "I will sell you this asset for a payment of this amount over this period of time unless I die, in which case no further payments are due."

What this technique does for estate taxes is that it removes any future payments due to the seller from the estate taxes owed at the time of death.

It may be tempting to abuse this technique for an interfamily sale strictly to avoid estate tax for a "land-rich, cash-poor" family. It is highly recommended to discuss this technique with a qualified estate planning attorney.

A SCIN would look something like the following:

Mary Beth is 68 years old and has recently been widowed. She has four children, all of whom are in their early fifties. She is the grandmother to eight and great-grandmother to two. Mary Beth now has full ownership of all of the assets she and her husband have accumulated over their lives. These assets include a mobile home park and about a dozen rental properties.

Mary Beth and her husband had a living trust, but now that property values have risen so sharply, she has become aware that she owns too much property, but she likes having all of the income her mobile home park and rentals provide. However, with such a large family, she feels that it is her duty to keep as much in the family as possible. With a net worth of over $8 million dollars, Mary Beth has a significant estate and is not easily insurable due to her age.

She consulted an estate planning attorney and decided to start selling her rental properties to each of her kids through Self-Canceling Installment Notes.

Each of her four children is willing to "buy" two rental homes at fair market value apiece and make monthly payments to their mother for the next 20 years unless she dies, in which case no further payments are due.

In this scenario, Mary Beth passes on the trouble of managing most of the rental homes to her children but still receives the monthly income she likes to have. Part of each payment she receives will be taxable as capital gains, but only as she receives it. No bank is involved, as Mary Beth is doing the financing.

Since the rental homes have been sold to her children, they are outside of her taxable estate when she dies. In most cases, the full capital gains due from the sale of each rental home will be paid by Mary Beth's estate when she passes on, but by transferring present interest and disregarding future interest, her taxable estate is greatly reduced.

Again, please consult with qualified estate planning advisors, financial advisors, and CPAs when exploring this technique, as it should be a coordinated group effort to get the best results.

Now let's take a look at a Private Annuity Contract*.

A Private Annuity Contract has all of the same features and benefits as a SCIN. This means that it can defer payment of Capital Gains Taxes as each payment is received. It also means that just like a SCIN, the future interest of an asset is removed from a seller's estate and is somewhat sheltered from the death tax.

Where a SCIN says, "Pay me this payment for this amount of time unless I die, then no further payments are due." a Private Annuity Contract* says, "Pay me this amount of money for as long as I am alive, and then no further payments are due."

See the difference? A Private Annuity Contract* is based on mortality instead of a set term. Mortality is determined by consulting an actuarial table in use by insurance companies, thus the term "Private Annuity*."

The use of a qualified estate planning attorney is highly recommended to distinguish whether a Private Annuity Contract* or a SCIN is most appropriate. It is generally the case that the older the seller is, the more likely a Private Annuity Contract* will be used instead of a SCIN.

Intent is the key operative with Private Annuity Contracts* and SCINs. I believe it is safe to say that the intent of either of these strategies would be to reduce estate taxes and that the deferral of a Capital

Gains Tax would be of secondary importance. However, it could also be said that if a younger seller did not require large installment-style payments, a Private Annuity Contract* might be of greater value.

For example, a seller in his middle 50s could collect smaller installment payments over a much longer period of time by using a Private Annuity Contract*. This seller could also legally "give a break" to a son or daughter with cash flow concerns and help teach responsibility by selling them a property through a Private Annuity Contract*.

On the other hand, if Mary Beth, from the last example, was 78 years old instead of 68 years old, there is a very good chance that a Private Annuity Contract would be used instead of a SCIN. This is because the likelihood of Mary Beth living to age 98 could be challenged if her expected mortality was only 86. Who would challenge this? The IRS and the result could be an unexpected estate tax or gift tax if the challenge was successful.

Unfortunately, this would mean higher payments made to Mary Beth from her children based on the shorter term of mortality (10 years) vs 20 years in a SCIN.

Often, families will try to be creative with these techniques, and the only comment that can be reasonably made is that the more creative a family becomes, the greater the likelihood of the strategy being challenged and penalized or otherwise declared a sham transaction.

The next page shows a brief chart on the pros and cons of each basic installment sale technique. Mary Beth's Self Canceling Installment Note and Private Annuity Contract*:

Mary Beth has a large family and wishes to pass her income-producing rental properties to her kids. Each child of Mary Beth will make fair market value payments to Mary

Beth for 30 years or until she dies. If Mary Beth dies, then her children will stop making payments. Each of these techniques has the same treatment for Capital Gains Tax as an Installment sale, but the benefits for estate tax are far greater.

For this illustration, we will assume each rental property was purchased for $40,000.00 (remember, Mary Beth has 12 of these) and is currently worth $400,000.00. Since this is required to be a fair market value transaction, we will assume a 6% interest rate charged to each child on the sale of each rental. We will also assume the current positive cash flow of $1,400.00 per month from each rental. We will also assume no mortgage is present on each property

	KEEP THE PROPERTY	NORMAL SALE	SCIN	PRIVATE ANNUITY*	PRO/CON
SALE PRICE OF 2 RENTAL Properties	Can Mortgage up to 80%. Mary Beth could 'borrow out' about $640,000.00 from any two rentals but would then have negative cash flow for mortgage payments.	Gross $800,000.00	$800.000.00 balance earning interest through installment-like payments for a period of time unless death occurs.	The $800,000.00 balance is earning interest through installment-like payments for life.	A SCIN is for a fixed period of time or until the demise of the seller. A Private Annuity is for the lifetime of the seller. The amount of payments will vary from technique to technique based on the age of the seller.
TAX OWED	None	$174,960.00	$174,960.00 deferred as each payment is made.	$174,960.00 deferred as each payment is made.	Generally, the ability to defer a tax payment is a good thing.
DEPRECIATION RECAPTURE?	None	Estimate $10,000.00 each	Estimate $10,000.00 each	Estimate $10,000.00 each	Depreciation may limit utility of strategy
AMOUNT MARY BETH RECEIVES FROM SALE	None	$605,040.00	Monthly payments are estimated at $2,400.00 for each rental.	Monthly payments depend on age Estimate: $2,900.00 or $4,525.00 for each rental.	A large portion of each monthly payment will be Capital Gains Taxable.

	KEEP THE PROPERTY	NORMAL SALE	SCIN	PRIVATE ANNUITY*	PRO/CON
HOW DOES IT AFFECT THE ESTATE?	The full value of each $400,000.00 rental could be estate taxable.	A lump sum of after-sale proceeds could be estate taxable.	Each property sold is removed from the estate. The estate is drained of $4.8 million if all rentals are sold.	Each property sold is removed from the estate. The estate is drained of about $4.8 million if all rentals are sold.	The estate is saved from about $2.4 million in projected estate tax; however, each child now has a negative cash flow property for as long as Mary Beth is alive.
INCOME RECEIVED?	$1,400.00 per month each. The total annual gross is approximately $33,600.00.	Lump sum invested at 6% return for income of $36,302.00 without depleting principal.	For a 30-year SCIN, Mary Beth would receive about $2,400.00 per month from each rental. This would be about $57,600.00 gross annually.	Mary Beth @ 68 would receive $2,900.00 per month. At age 78, she receives $4,525.00 per month. This would be $69,600.00 annually or $108,600.00 annual gross.	Income for Mary Beth increases in all situations. For a SCIN or Private Annuity, the kids would have to make payments but would ultimately avoid estate tax concerns.

The bottom line is that a SCIN or a Private Annuity* is a transaction that requires competent legal and tax advice to perform, and it does lessen the impact of paying Capital Gains Tax to a degree; however, the benefit for estate tax could be much greater as the payments made to Mary Beth only continue for as long as she is alive. Normally, these techniques are only used for Intra-Family sales, but they can apply to any sort of asset. Depreciation recapture costs are not addressed by this technique in most cases. Please remember that due to current IRS regulations, a Private Annuity may not have any capital gains deferral benefits after October 2006

LIKE-KIND EXCHANGES:
The 1031 Exchange

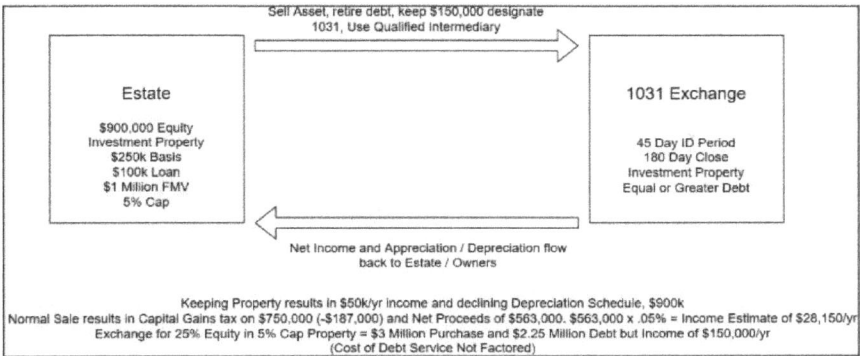

The 1031 Exchange is one of the most commonly used real estate growth tools. It allows for the taxable portion of a sale of one property to be carried over to the purchase of a replacement property. We will just list a few of the Basics of a 1031 Exchange and then spend some time on what to do when they go wrong!

Requirements for a 1031 Exchange

• Property exchanged must have been held for trade, business, or investment

- Includes residential (if held for investment), commercial, and raw land assets
- Excludes stocks, bonds, and other certificates of trust or beneficial interests

- Cannot take constructive receipt of money on the sale of property
  - Retain a Qualified Intermediary (Accommodator)

- Must replace property with the same or greater value of the relinquished property
  - Can replace existing debt with a greater cash investment
  - Cannot replace cash with greater debt (the excess cash will be taxed)

- Must identify replacement property within 45 days of close on relinquished property

- Must acquire new asset within 180 days of closing on the relinquished property

DEFINITIONS:

Qualified Intermediary (QI)

The facilitator of a 1031 exchange. Also known as an Accommodator. The QI takes constructive receipt of exchange funds, acts as a principal of an exchange, and prepares the legal documentation.

Constructive Receipt

Taking control of the proceeds from the liquidation of an investment real estate asset. Personally taking receipt of proceeds will negate your exchangeability.

Like-Kind Property

Refers to the nature or character of property relinquished and purchased as replacement, not grade.

Boot

Non-qualified funds or property received in an exchange. Also, any unspent funds or non- replaced debt will be taxed as boot.

Identification Period (ID Period)

The period of time in which possible replacement properties must be chosen. ID Period begins at the close of escrow of the relinquished property and ends on the 45th day following. No extensions for weekends or holidays.

Exchange Period

The period of time in which the replacement property must be acquired, and all exchange funds must be exhausted. The exchange period begins at the close of escrow of the relinquished property and ends on the 180th day following. No extensions for weekends or holidays. The Exchange Period runs concurrently with the ID Period and, therefore, ends 135 days following the end of the ID Period.

1031 EXCHANGE CASE STUDY:

Jim is planning on selling an investment property. His goal is to not pay the tax and to continue to invest in real estate. Jim is 45 and could manage the new property if he had to.

Jim is the perfect candidate for a 1031 Exchange.

Jim has an investment property to sell, and he wants to keep building his list of real estate positions. He currently manages several properties and does not mind managing more.

In this scenario, we will assume Jim has a $400,000.00 property he purchased 5 years ago for $200,000.00. He currently owes $160,000.00 for a mortgage, and the property has a positive cash flow of about $100.00 per month. Jim wants to move into a 4 plex worth about $800,000, and he will place all $240,000.00 of equity towards the purchase. After figuring out the numbers, Jim will increase his cash flow from this transaction to about $600.00 per month.

THE 1031 EXCHANGE:

	NORMAL SALE	1031 EXCHANGE	PRO/CON
SALE PRICE	$400,000.00	$400,000.00	By doing the Exchange, Jim is really borrowing an extra $400,000.00.
TAX OWED	$50,000.00	$50,000.00 is deferred until the sale of the new property.	With a 1031 Exchange, Jim does not have to give up money to the government.
DEPRECIATION RECAPTURED?	Whatever Jim has Depreciated will be charged an additional tax.	Probably not; would depend on Jim's Tax advisor and the amount depreciated.	Generally, a 1031 Exchange will avoid Depreciation recapture costs.
AMOUNT JIM RECEIVES FROM SALE	About $190,000.00 after tax and debt.	Jim buys an income of about $600.00 per month plus possible future appreciation.	Obviously, in this example, a 1031 Exchange is more attractive than a normal sale.
HOW DOES IT AFFECT THE ESTATE?	The $190,000.00 is in the Estate.	The new 4-plex is in the Estate.	If Jim dies, his wife will keep this income asset.

The bottom line is that a 1031 Exchange is the best way to grow a real estate position because any tax that might be payable is deferred until the actual asset is later sold. Most of this eBook is dedicated to those investors who have decided that a 1031 Exchange is probably not the best fit for their long-term needs or are looking for a higher positive cash flow than available replacement properties. Some readers may be looking for a way to avoid 1031 Exchange requirements or have a 1031 Rescue in place before starting a planned 1031 Exchange in case something goes wrong.

1031 EXCHANGE INTO A SECTION 721 (UP-REIT)

A relatively new development in the world of 1031 Exchangeable assets includes what is being called an Up-REIT. A REIT stands for a Real Estate Investment Trust and can be thought of as a sort of 'mutual fund' of real estate-related assets or notes secured by real estate assets.

Now, when someone does a 1031 Exchange, it is a Like Kind Exchange. This means that if you have an investment property, you can exchange it for another investment property and not pay the tax. It does not mean you can exchange an investment property for a REIT. (Though you can, in fact, exchange one property for multiple properties or exchange multiple properties for one property).

An Up-REIT actually uses two different sections of the current tax code that effectively allow an investor to exchange an investment property for a highly diversified REIT, but it has some rules.

Essentially, you would do a 1031 Exchange into a Tenants in Common or Special Purpose LLC project that was under contract to be acquired by a REIT. You will generally hold the investment for a period of at least one year, and then when the REIT acquires the project you purchased, you are given REIT partnership units in exchange for your Limited Stock Ownership of the Tenants in Common project.

This process is called an Up-REIT, presumably because you cannot 1031 Exchange into a REIT, but you can change the class of ownership from LLC units to Partnership Units while also deferring the tax.

Here is the catch: Though you have acquired a very diversified real estate investment position, you will not be able to perform a 1031 exchange again when the REIT closes that door. You would still have opportunities to use other techniques in this eBook, though, such as a Charitable trust variant or even the Model Q™ Installment Trust.

The amount of "ifs" that have to occur for a successful Section 721 Up-REIT to function as advertised means that this technique is *not really something for the average investor* but more of a marketing pitch by REIT companies looking to expand…so be very careful of your math with the replacement REIT and read all of the agreements.

The only positive angle is that REITs have to publicly report everything, which means they do have to tell you how you overpay. Frequently, additional costs are layered into the 'Partner Firms" of the REIT; however, unless it is for a fixed price, there is potential for abuse. Ownership rights of REIT units vary widely, but generally speaking, there is very limited control one has...a REIT is truly a passive investment and is illiquid to boot. We are discussing Non-Public REITs sold by Private Placement Memorandum and not the Publicly Traded REITs that are available in the stock market, different animals entirely and for a Section 721 UpREIT you will only have access to Closed REITs sold by PPM.

Up-REITs are, again, fairly new investment tools and are fairly complex transactions. Very few UP- REITs have reliable third-party due diligence performed to determine legitimacy in following Tax Code guidelines to ensure a tax-deferred transaction— this is often disclosed as the buyer's responsibility. At this point in time, Up-REITs should be investigated with great care, though it would be a terrific strategy for someone who wanted to stay invested in real estate in a very diversified manner and did not want to deal with tenants and who wanted to create or expand a REIT and take on additional property owners.

In the author's opinion, there are better tools available for selling an appreciated asset to get an income than an Up-REIT.

THE 1031 EXCHANGE INTO A DELAWARE
Statutory Trust (DST)

We previously learned about the rules for a 1031 Exchange, Like property for Like property, and Equal or Greater debt is the summary. Now, it is not at all possible to exchange 1031 into a REIT or Real Estate Investment Trust directly, but it is possible to exchange 1031 into a Tenants in Common project with a limited number of owners and a third-party administrator. It is also possible to 1031 Exchange into a single Building about to be acquired by a REIT…which is the 721 UpReit previously discussed.

A Delaware Statutory Trust is a special Trust formed in such a way as to appear to have the benefits of a Real Estate Investment Trust but also the structure to allow a 1031 Exchange to be performed.

DSTs were mostly allowed with some substantial caveats by Rev Ruling 2004-86.

The Caveats to a DST are as follows:

1. Once the offering is closed, there can be no future contributions to the DST by either current or new beneficiaries.

2. The trustee cannot renegotiate the terms of the existing loans and cannot borrow any new funds from any party unless a loan default exists as a result of a tenant bankruptcy or insolvency.

3. The trustee cannot reinvest the proceeds from the sale of its real estate.

4. The trustee is limited to making capital expenditures with respect to the property for normal repair and maintenance, minor nonstructural capital improvements, and those required by law.

5. Any reserves or cash held between distribution dates can only be invested in short-term debt obligations.

6. All cash, other than necessary reserves, must be distributed on a current basis.

7. The trustee cannot enter into new leases or renegotiate the current leases unless there is a need due to a tenant's bankruptcy or insolvency.

Like many things in life...if you have to try very, very, very hard to accomplish a task that should be simple, you have to wonder if you are doing something wrong. DSTs appear to try really, really hard to satisfy 1031 Exchange Guidelines while also giving an Income solution that is diversified over many properties with many other owners as a replacement property, but at a cost so great as to make a DST more of a sales pitch than a viable solution.

One has to wonder how anyone actually approves of a DST purchase when they know what they are getting into. There is not only a 100% lack of control…but the DST cannot renegotiate leases nor will it sell any non-performing properties….and if it does happen to be 'forced' to sell a property, then the proceeds must be held in cash or other short term debt instruments?

Does this sound like something any fiduciary professional would recommend to any client? Is this even a strategy to consider, or is it actually just a sales pitch?

We are just talking about a simple structure. While it is certainly possible that a DST may have such a great portfolio of underlying investments that it is just superior, it would have to be truly fantastic to give up so much so as to make the deal happen.

We have already covered knowing how to ask the right questions to help select a tax-advantaged strategy. Let us go through and try to make a 1031 Exchange into a DST solution in some fashion.

Our right question would likely resemble, "I want to sell this property and get higher income as well as a tax advantage to capital gains." Seems like a fair assumption. So we know it is mostly an Income position, as opposed to appreciation potential, that drives an inquiry into a 1031/DST.

So, what does a DST pay, and how reliable is the income? That is a great question. I think it is safe to assume that with a DST, just like a REIT, the ownership cost is slightly higher to pay the Trustee and administration costs. Even if the administration costs do not grow over time, the Leases will eventually expire, or the businesses will change, and the DST will earn less as vacancies grow without new tenants being approved.

Not to mention normal maintenance or unusually expensive maintenance that has to be paid for somewhere...but if the costs exceed cash reserves, well, they have to get paid somewhere, and new debt cannot be renegotiated.

Need liquidity? Well, you have to wait for the Trustee to close the DST.

So we can get into a DST for income...but that income is at the highest it will ever be as soon as you 1031 Exchange into the program. From then on, it will most likely be reduced.

Let's compare those observations to almost any other 1031 Exchange or gain tax deferral technique, and you quickly see that it simply does not measure up in any capacity unless there is some other issue outside of income that drives the consideration.

The author believes that in the case of 1031 into a DST... it is actually better to simply pay the gains tax owed if one is looking for an income solution and a Tax advantage.

Whereas a section 721 UpReit may have some utility, a DST has enough negative elements that it fails in comparison to every other possible strategy on multiple levels….unless some sort of outside consideration lends enough weight to the DST structure to offset the numerous drawbacks.

There is hardly any possible way that a Fiduciary could recommend a 1031/ DST and go over a formal comparison in a way that makes sense for any investor. It is simply too restrictive on all counts.

WHAT TO DO WHEN A 1031 EXCHANGE FAILS:

1031 Exchanges are complex creatures, even though they are fairly common. The trick with the 1031 Exchange is the timelines to close. Every Real Estate Investor knows that a property sale or purchase is not real until the very last signature has been signed and the check has been delivered! The 45-day replacement property period is not usually a problem, but the closing on the new purchase within 180 days frequently develops issues and is the cause of many failed 1031s. This can be negotiating the contract or having your financing fall through at the last moment.

A failed 1031 Exchange means you pay the tax on the already completed sale UNLESS you are wise and have a backup plan ALREADY in place.

The issue with a sale like this being approved or being disallowed lies in the planned execution of one tax code…completing the sale of the Property and listing the applicable tax code to bypass Taxable Gains recognition and then having the Qualified Intermediary return the funds to you directly because there is no replacement property.

As soon as the check is made out to you directly…, that is a constructive receipt, and that means you have lost all tax benefits; the sale is complete when you get that check.

Now, it is possibly arguable that this very fact is how 1031 into DSTs evolved…by trapping failed 1031 Exchanges in a Faustian bargain… but there is a better way!

To fix this situation, you <u>have to start</u> with finding a Qualified Intermediary that has a specialized Escrow agreement. They are out there but harder to find, and the nutshell version is that the Escrow Agreement you sign with the QI allows for a return of that Escrow balance held for the 1031 Exchange over time in the form of an Installment Sale — usually managed by a third party independent from the QI that also passes all of the Related Party requirements for the Installment Method as described by the Internal Revenue Code.

In fact— the Model Q™ Installment Sale Trust is usually selected for this by Qualified Intermediaries simply because it is revocable and managed by a third party. (Irrevocable Trusts are not normally considered useful in this fashion for two reasons: 1— because the intent of the Trust is clouded and 2— there is specific language that disallows Irrevocable Trusts to be used for escrowed funds in IRC 1031).

So- to address the possibility of a failed 1031, you need to start with the assumption that the 1031 will fail and get the right agreements before you close on the property you are selling. Ideally, you identify your partner QI well before you even consider selling.

THE 1042 EXCHANGE:

The only other "Like-Kind Exchange" this eBook covers is the 1042 Exchange. It's not nearly as common as a 1031 Exchange but possibly of interest for Business Owners and Real Estate Owners who hold an appreciated asset through a business structure. This is far less common in one sense but actually very common in another sense.

Whereas a 1031 Exchange is Like to Like for Investment Property/Assets, a 1042 Exchange allows for the Exchange of Privately-held Stock for Publicly-held Stock.

Remember, if you own a business that owns property or some other asset, you do not directly own the property or asset. Instead, you own shares of the business. With this technique, you can defer paying Capital Gains Tax on the sale of a business (or business asset) by collecting the cash from the sale, determining the new basis in company shares you own, and subsequently purchasing publicly traded stock, for example, dividend producing Blue Chips or shares from the S&P 500. Some Tax Advisors may even feel comfortable allowing a 1042 Exchange to invest in certain types of mutual funds or Exchange Traded Mutual Funds (ETFs) based on their interpretation of IRC Section 1042.

This is a very common technique used by large companies

making an acquisition. If you have seen in the newspapers a business sale for "X" amount of dollars and "Stock," you may be seeing a 1042 Exchange transaction in some form.

If you combine this with an Employee Stock Option Plan for a business owned by a family, you incidentally have a powerful estate planning technique to pass wealth to your heirs.

How is this done? Well, you have basically unitized the value of your business, and for gifting purposes to your heirs, you should have no trouble performing the maximum annual allowable gift of shares of stock without filing a gift tax return.

1042 Exchanges are simple in concept but complex in structure, so rather than go too far into the weeds, let's just look at an example.

Herb owns a business that repairs and rebuilds big rig diesel motors. Herb owns the business as a C– Corporation and 100% of the shares of the business after having bought out his partner five years ago. Herb is married but has no children. Herb is 62 and has always enjoyed investing in stocks. When he is getting ready to sell his business, his advisor tells him that it may be possible to perform a 1042 Exchange and put almost the entire amount of money he receives from the asset portion of the sale of his business as well as the land. With the 1042 Exchange, the business sale will turn into part cash and part Stock in the Buyer of his Business, a National Trucking and Shipping Company.

Herb immediately falls for the idea of not having to pay Capital Gains Tax until he sells or liquidates the stock shares in the Buyer that he acquires from his 1042 Exchange.

Herb's case study would consist of a business broker to help sell the business and his CPA to calculate all of the tax implications for the sale. Herb would also need to find a legal representative to ensure that his 1042 Exchange was correctly performed. Herb might use an Investment Advisor or Stockbroker to purchase his shares of Publicly Held stock, or he might choose to open his own self- directed brokerage account at an institution like E-Trade or Ameritrade.

The 1042 Exchange is usually for Publicly held stock of the acquisition company but maybe for a basket of stocks or a stock index ETF, depending on the situation!

s

A 1042 Exchange is a little (actually a lot) more complex than a 1031 Exchange and is not nearly as common for transactions under 20 Million, so legal costs would be much greater than with a 1031 Exchange, but it is still a very useful technique indeed for those who like to participate in the Stock Market.

THE IRREVOCABLE INSTALLMENT SALE TRUST:

Before we really dive into the Model Q™ Installment Sale Trust, let's take a look at the more common Irrevocable Installment Trust version. It is frequently called an Installment Sale Trust, Deferred Installment Sale Trust, or some version of Trust and Installment.

The key piece, both the greatest Strengths and greatest Weaknesses, is inside the structure.

The structure is an Irrevocable Trust, and therein lies all of the additional qualification hurdles.

The key elements of the Irrevocable Trust structure are that the Grantor loses complete control over the Trust and typically cannot change or even influence ANY elements of the Trust after its creation. The Grantor can also, therefore, by definition, not be the Trustee nor a related party to the Trustee. There are also a series of ongoing tests for control that really limit ANY involvement in ANY process the Grantor has in the Irrevocable Trust once it is created and funded.

It is supposed to be 100% Hands-Off once you make the election. Hence the term "Irrevocable".

The good part of this structure is that whatever is held in the Trust can be removed from the Grantor's estate, which also has significant Asset Protection connotations. Also, when done properly, the Assets held in the Trust are 100% belonging to the Beneficiaries of the Trust.

So, when you add an Installment Note variant into an Irrevocable Trust structure, you end up with a way to Sell an Appreciated Asset like Real Estate or the Asset portion of a Business and defer the tax owed at sale through the Installment Method while still collecting all of the money from the buyer upfront.

The differences between irrevocable and revocable installment trusts deal with ownership and influence tests to retain 100% of the money and increase audit risk, but there is no difference in tax advantages.

Revocable and Irrevocable Installment Trust Diagram:

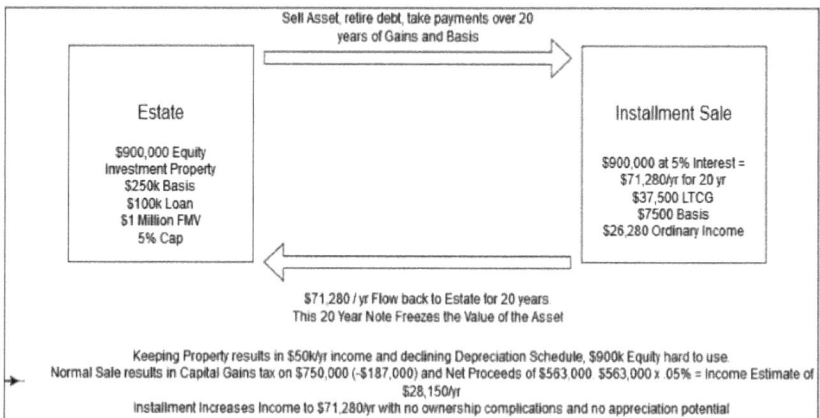

A Family Trust or Inter-Vivos Trust is a grantor trust, which means that the owners of the trust retain full rights to change the trust, which is a topic further explored in the "Just Say No" eBook for Estate Planning coming soon from Q Financial.

For an Irrevocable Trust variant of some kind with an Installment Note, in short, you establish your Non-Grantor Trust, and since it has an EIN number, it becomes a legal entity. You then sell your property to your Non-Grantor Trust in exchange for a repayment schedule that dictates the terms of repayment you expect from your Trust.

At this point, your Trust has a piece of property and an obligation or promise to pay to make payments back to the Grantor(s). The Trust then has to have cash to make those payments, so the Trust becomes the 'seller' in the escrow process and will take the seller's place when dealing with the buyer of your property.

If you have a 1 million dollar piece of property that you sell to your Trust for an installment-like payment, and your Trust then sells the same property to the buyer for 1 million dollars in exchange for cash...guess what? Your Trust bought the property for 1 million dollars and sold the property for 1 million dollars. There are no "capital gains" for the sale made by the Trust.

Instead, every payment the Trust makes back to the Grantor(s) has a return of Capital Gains Taxable income based on the ability to correctly qualify for the Installment Method treatment for Capital Gains Taxes discussed in IRC 453.

Remember, your Non-Grantor Trust is a separate legal entity with its own EIN number. You might have any sort of Installment Note Contract making your payments; there is no direct guidance from the IRS on contract terms. The Installment Method simply states that as you receive the money, you are taxed. Self Canceling notes, interest-only notes, and even Options may be allowable if correctly structured.

Keep in mind that the asset you sold to your Trust is now effectively removed from your taxable estate, and the payments you enjoy are designed to last for an extended period of time, often decades. Also, keep in mind that Capital Gains Tax planning for incomes under a certain amount is actually free of tax! With careful planning of installment terms, it is actually possible to eliminate and not just defer the long-term Capital Gains Tax if one seeks a zero-gains tax situation or needs to qualify for certain welfare or benefit programs that are income-based.

Other strategies that follow a similar philosophy but are primarily designed for inter-family sales and utilize gift tax exclusions include primary residence grantor-retained interest trusts, grantor-retained annuity trusts, and intentionally defective grantor trusts. You may have also heard of Family Limited Partnerships.

These types of strategies generally have no Capital Gains Tax "benefits" but still serve an important role in addressing estate tax. We will look briefly at each of these techniques and cover them more thoroughly in the Just Say No eBook for Estate Planning, but due to the lack of significant Capital Gains Tax advantages, they will not really be covered in this eBook.

Let's take a look at a case study:

Dean is 61 years old, and his wife, Melissa, is 57. They are going to sell a ranch and move to something smaller, a little closer to their kids. Dean and Melissa are concerned about paying taxes and having enough income for retirement. Dean wants to retire in 4 years.

After reviewing a 1031 Exchange strategy, Dean and Melissa are uncomfortable with having "all of their eggs in one basket" for their retirement income. They decide that an Installment Sale held in an Irrevocable Trust would best fit their goals. They will hold all of the money from the ranch sale in their trust for 5 years. In the fifth year, the trust will start making payments of about $45,000 per year for as long as Dean and Melissa for a term not to exceed 20 years.

The Irrevocable Trust Installment Sale makes sense to Dean and Melissa as they are planning several years in advance and want to really provide for their kids in a meaningful fashion.

In this example, Dean and Melissa are able to exchange their ranch for a respectable income payment at a future sale date. This income will help supplement their retirement until the 20-year scheduled term expires.

When Dean and Melissa pass away, the assets in the irrevocable trust are immediately passed to their kids without going through probate. Keep in mind that the Capital Gains Tax does not disappear; if Dean and Melissa die before they have paid their capital gains bill to Uncle Sam, then the remaining part of that tax bill is usually immediately payable and will be handled by their executor or executrix, but the Irrevocable Trust is/may be handled by a third party Trustee, and if the Trust terms state the beneficiaries, then a death certificate will trigger the inheritance.

It is that simple.

Since the Trust is held outside of Dean and Melissa's estate, it is somewhat protected from judgments, liens, and possible bankruptcy claims. This means that this trust will continue making payments as long as money is available in the trust, as long as the Term is required, and as long as the income beneficiaries are intact.

It is important to note that Non-grantor trusts are very complex animals, frequently beyond the understanding of financial advisors and CPAs alike, and really do require an experienced Estate Planner and not just an Estate Planner with a template document.

This example only serves to highlight the end result of a successful Irrevocable Trust paired with correct Installment terms and assumes a long list of rules are followed and that Dean and Melissa are comfortable with the drawbacks of the Irrevocable strategy.

All things considered, any Irrevocable Trust variant that holds an Installment Contract should be started with the intent to exchange a highly appreciated asset "for a lifetime income" and for "estate tax benefits or to help create a legacy." Capital gains advantages should be of secondary importance because of the Irrevocable nature of the structure. That is really where the Model Q™ Installment Sale Trust has a tremendous advantage because it absolutely can be structured specifically as a tax advantage and without the related tests for intent that follow the Estate Planning doctrine. The Model Q™ IST is simpler, but the drawback is that any Revocable Structure lacks the same gifting capacity as an Irrevocable Trust Structure.

With all Installment Sale Trust Variants, I want to let you in on a fact that is not widely known or understood. It is part of what makes these Trusts terrific tools to work with during the present day. The repayment terms are based on current interest rates. I might also point out that interest rates are currently very close to the lowest point they have been in about 40 years. What that tells me as a portfolio manager is that chances are very high that the interest rates will rise again, and when they do, it will then be possible to outperform expectations.

For now, let me remind you that a competent advisor is needed to fully explore the benefits and drawbacks of both ALL types of non-grantor and irrevocable trusts.

Case Study – Dean and Melissa's Irrevocable Installment Trust:

Dean and Melissa bought their ranch for $100,000.00 in the 1980's. It is currently worth about 1.5 million. Since it was their primary residence, they have an exclusion of $500,000.00 in Capital Gains Tax. They have no debt on this property.

	NORMAL SALE	IRREVOCABLE INSTALLMENT TRUST	PRO/CON
SALE PRICE	$1.5 Million	$1.5 Million	Dean and Melissa can collect the full sales price and provide a comfortable retirement income without paying a chunk of money to Uncle Sam at the sale.
TAX OWED	$218,700.00	$218,7000.00 is deferred and is partially payable as each payment is made.	Interest earned on Deferred Taxes is good. Being locked into that income stream is Irrevocable.
DEPRECIATION RECAPTURED?	Yes, but since this is a primary residence, it is treated a little differently.	Deferred as each payment is made, a part may be recaptured.	N/A
AMOUNT RECEIVED FROM SALE	About $1,281,300.00 after tax. This would create about $76,878.00 annual income at 6% without depleting the principal.	Income payments would be about $111,888.00 annually for as long as Dean and Melissa were alive.	Higher payments are structured to last for a term and may continue after the installment term.

| HOW DOES IT AFFECT THE ESTATE? | The $1,281,300.00 is in the Estate. | The full sale price of $1.5 million is removed from the taxable estate and is held in Trust for heirs. | When Dean and Melissa both die, the heirs inherit everything remaining in the Trust. The Trust is not part of the taxable estate, but the income owed to Dean and Melissa may be part of the Taxable estate. |

The bottom line is that a 1031 Exchange is the best way to grow a real estate position because any tax that might be payable is deferred until the actual asset is later sold. Most of this eBook is dedicated to those investors who have decided that a 1031 Exchange is probably not the best fit for their long-term needs or are looking for a higher positive cash flow than available replacement properties. Some readers may be looking for a way to avoid 1031 Exchange requirements or have a 1031 Rescue in place before starting a planned 1031 Exchange in case something goes wrong.

THE MODEL Q™ STRUCTURED INSTALLMENT SALE

So now we get to explain a little extra about our flagship offering and how it differs from all of the more commonly found irrevocable trust installment variables. The Model Q™ Structured Installment Sale was designed after decades of experience with all of the other forms of tax-advantaged structures that are explained in this eBook.

In those decades of combined experiences, everyone at Q Financial has seen abuses and failed structures many times over.

We have seen Irrevocable Installment Trusts mismanaged by Trustees for Profit and Commissions with no recourse. We have seen hundreds of failed 1031 Exchanges. We have seen a lot of Charitable trusts and Private Non-Profits created, and then the Grantors try to buy back assets or influence the recipient Charity or even just make a simple mistake in Grant writing and Unrelated Business Taxable Income or bookkeeping, just purely clerical errors that cause the Charitable Trust and even the Non- Profit to implode....and it usually blows back directly on the Grantors as previously allowed tax advantages are disallowed and reassessed with penalties and interest.

Lawyers and specialists that work with these other Gains Deferral or Elimination techniques are 'usually' fully aware of all of the pitfalls of their chosen strategy, 'usually' give great advice, and 'usually' have very tight language in their agreements and reporting. The largest Non-Profits have their own internal legal teams and often also have very tight processes.

The problems, however, always seem to come from innocent error or grantor self-sabotage when a better deal or some other life-changing circumstance comes along after an Irrevocable Election is made.

I don't want to give the impression that every other tax-advantaged strategy in this book is inferior or always breaks, but in our collective experience… every other Tax Advantage certainly has significant risks and complications in excess of the Model Q™ Structured Installment Sale. They do not ALWAYS work, and there is very often no recourse at all for a failed transaction or a transaction that loses an advantage over time for whatever reason.

The Model Q™ SIS addresses every failure point we have ever seen and always seems to simply
work.

The trick lies in the fact that it is set up with a Revocable Trust and has a Business Purpose… which is Profit Sharing. As long as the Grantors that create the Trust are willing to "Share the Profit of the Management of the Trust

Assets" past the installment sale terms with a non-related Third Party, then all normal failure points are simply and elegantly addressed.

It brings to mind an older saying that goes something like "Pigs get Fat, but Hogs get Slaughtered," meaning if you try to get too greedy, it eventually catches up with you.

Every other tax advantage strategy for capital gains deferral that this eBook covers has some weird complications, and those complications can be for a single transaction or can last for decades of reporting.

Even the very best tool for Real Estate growth, the 1031 Exchange, seems to force bad purchases for the unwary or pressured investor more often than it does not within the Exchange-required timelines and property profiles.

The amount of disallowed Charitable Trusts and court cases behind them are more than staggering…it is actually monumental. Thousands to tens of thousands have been disallowed or penalized!

All that being said, people are people, and we all want the best deal we can get, and we are all actually legally entitled to the best tax advantage that we can deploy

When you get to a certain point in life, however, you realize the meaning behind that saying, "Pigs get Fat, and

Hogs get Slaughtered." Jumping through a hoop or two is fine…jumping through 20-30 hoops every year for the rest of your life should be very calculated and worth the effort. Mr Murphy, aka Murphy's Law, seems to exploit any given weakness allowed, and if your plan requires attention to multiple potential failure points, just make sure it is worth the risk.

The best choices seem to involve having as many people behind you as you can get to work together for a common purpose with the least amount of liability. You assemble a team of like- minded professionals who can keep each other in check and deliver a superior, custom-tailored end result with limited risk of the strategy blowing up. This actually describes every technique mentioned in this eBook as long as the professionals who are hired do their jobs and work well together.

The very, very best choices also directly limit your own ability to sabotage yourself while also allowing for enough control for a 180-degree switch at any point in time for any reason. This second part is nearly impossible to accomplish with a Tax Advantage; in fact, there is only ONE WAY to do it, and that is because Q Financial created it.

A Third Party Revocable Installment Trust with Profit Sharing.

That is the Model Q™ Structured Installment Sale.

This Trust is just like the Irrevocable Installment Trust previously discussed, except for two key points. It involves Profit Sharing of Trust performance over the Installment note contract. Oh, and the Revocable part means you can 'opt-out' of the Trust and Installment note and just pay a penalty similar to a Bank CD and Pay any remaining Capital Gains Tax. You get all of the contractual protections you need to get a Tax Advantage, and you retain enough control to opt-out, which is something you do not find...literally in every other strategy you have available.

Once you pull the trigger with ANY other technique, then you bear the consequences. There is no do-over. Just to rephrase...if you do a 1031 exchange successfully and you get a substandard property with a lot of deferred maintenance, or the transaction fails...you are stuck. If you perform an Irrevocable Trust variant with an Installment note and you change your mind about any of the particulars for family, health, or business reasons...you are stuck. If you do a Charitable Trust variant and change your mind or want to redeploy assets held in your Trust...you are stuck.

Those are all Irrevocable elections once funded.

The Model Q™ Structured Installment Sale functions just like the Irrevocable Trust variant previously discussed except...well, do-overs and re-negotiations or extensions or changes are actually allowed.

The Seller (Grantor) sells an appreciated asset to a

Revocable Trust managed by a non-related third party. That Trust then drafts an installment sale note to the Grantor for a term and interest rate. The Capital Gains Tax that would normally be owed in the year of the sale is allowed treatment from the Installment Method, which means that a proportional amount of tax is owed as the payments are received.

Both the Asset and Installment Note are held outside of the Estate of the Seller/Grantor, which offers significant asset protections, and again, the value of the asset is frozen to the terms of the sum of the installments over time. After the end of the installment note term, any residual profits are shared with the Seller/Grantor instead of remaining 100% with the Seller/Grantor.

Model Q™ Structured Installment Sale Case Study

	NORMAL SALE	MODEL Q™ STRUCTURED INSTALLMENT SALE	PRO/CON
SALE PRICE	$1.5 Million	$1.5 Million	Dean and Melissa can collect the full sales price and provide a comfortable retirement income without paying a chunk of money to Uncle Sam at the sale.
TAX OWED	$218,700.00	$218,7000.00 is deferred and is partially payable as each payment is made.	
DEPRECIATION RECAPTURED?	Yes, but since this is a primary residence, it is a little different.	Yes, but again, as a personal residence	N/A
AMOUNT RECEIVED FROM SALE	About $1,281,300.00 after tax. This would create about $76,878.00 annual income at 6% without depleting the principal .	Income payments would be about $111,888.00 annually for a maximum of 20 years.	Instead of a traditional Installment sale, Dean and Melissa collect the full sales price and pay themselves their Installment payments. Profits from the Trust are split between the 3rd party Trustee and the Family. This allows the Installment and the Trust to be fully Revocable at any time.

HOW DOES IT AFFECT THE ESTATE?	The $1,281,300.00 is in the Estate..	The full sale price of $1.5 million is included in the estate.	The only positive effect is to 'freeze' the value of the estate to prevent future growth and a potential higher estate tax.

The bottom line is that the Model Q™ SIS is another very flexible technique to defer Capital Gains Tax and is almost exactly the same as the many Irrevocable Installment Trust variants. It can also be pre-designated as a 1031 Exchange rescue mechanism for a failed 1031 Exchange where an Irrevocable Installment Trust cannot be due to Trust Intent and specific IRS language. The other difference is that Trust profits experienced over the Installment Term are split instead of retained for the Grantors and Family. This allows for a Business Purpose and a Revocable aspect so that the Grantors can cancel the Trust or make significant changes without running afoul of the ownership and control tests that an Irrevocable Trust has.

THE CB FARMERS TRUST DELAWARE STATUTORY TRUST PROGRAM (DSTP)

The DSTP is a highly engineered product that is designed specifically for small farms and agricultural businesses to take advantage of tax code provisions that have only been practical for very large and publicly traded operations due to their complexity and expense.

What the CB Farmers Trust DSTP does is allow for the deferral of capital gains for a crop or farm sale while also giving the farmer a program to borrow most of that money back immediately.

What it looks like is the Seller sells the crop or asset and gets to defer the tax over a long period of time while having immediate access to over 95% of the post-sale proceeds. When it is set up for a Farmer, all that Farmer needs to do to manage the program is to collect money from sale proceeds held in Trust and use those same proceeds to partially offset a loan payment to a bank.

This means that this season's tax money owed on the crop or herd can be immediately leveraged back into the next season. If you are selling all or a part of a farming or agriculture business, it means you can use the Tax money owed before paying it to the Government. This program offers you a unique tax advantage, which, of course, may mean a huge difference in capability when margins are tight.

The tax code calls this a Monetized Installment Sale, and there is particular language directly from the IRS that allows for these transactions for a precisely defined agricultural business that basically does not process an end product for sale but instead provides the materials.

The Delaware Statutory Trust structure, in this instance, allows for a master agreement to cover many farmers (we told you this program had a layer of complexity!) Because the terms are always the same, the lender is always the same, and the program always requires US government bonds to be held in trust for the Lender to lend money back. The margin for profitability is also very small, so crafting a workable solution needs to be very streamlined indeed.

The Delaware Statutory Trust structure is a terrific structure, though it fails miserably when it is attempted to be used to satisfy 1031 Exchange guidelines, as previously explained in the 1031 to DST section of this eBook. The DST structure itself, however, is perfectly adapted for installment sales, installment method tax deferral, and even monetized installment programs!

Basically, to get the CB DSTP to work for tax liabilities of less than a million dollars (for small Farms and Ag services), it had to really be thought through and fine-tuned...but that being said, here is an example of a Private Transaction from a publicly traded company that also performed a monetized installment sale (and was publicly recognized for the technique) so you can see the power of a correctly structured Monetized Installment Sale and learn why Q Financial felt that there was absolutely a market for a small scale production of the very same tool.

Q Financial feels that a direct quote from the Journal of Corporation Taxation (WG&L) Nov/Dec 2004 is the best way to unpack how Monetized Installment Programs can be structured for very large transactions. The Author of this article from 2004 is Robert S Bernstein, partner at Foley and Lardner, LLP (which is a large law firm still in the business twenty years later, and the firm is known for working with renewable power, oil and gas, and more).

"The Boise Cascade Corporation

On 7/26/04, Boise Cascade Corp. announced that it had reached a definitive agreement to sell its paper, forest products, and timberland assets for approximately $3.7 billion to Madison Dearborn Partners, Inc., a private equity investment firm located in Chicago, Illinois.

Boise Cascade Corp. will change its company and trade name to OfficeMax shortly after the close of the transaction. Of the assets sold, approximately $1.65 billion of the purchase consideration is being delivered in the form of installment obligations for the timber properties. The balance of the transaction *proceeds will be paid in cash. Boise Cascade will use its tax basis in its non-timber properties and approximately $100 million worth of net operating loss carry-forwards to eliminate much of the gain on the cash portion of the transaction.*

In a conference call, Boise Cascade indicated that its tax basis in the timberlands "is quite low relative to today's market values."

The installment obligations will be secured by standby letters of credit issued by one or more banks. Liquid or other substantial assets will be deposited by Madison Dearborn Partners as collateral with the issuing banks to secure the banks against a draw under the standby letters of credit. The interest rate payable under the installment obligations will be equal to the rate of return payable on the collateral, less the costs associated with the standby letters of credit. <u>Boise Cascade will then pledge the installment obligation to one or more lending institutions as collateral for a loan equal to 90% of its face amount.</u>

Boise Cascade will reinvest approximately $175 million of the gross proceeds received by Boise.

Cascade, L.L.C. and its affiliates, the entities formed by Madison Dearborn Partners, to acquire the paper, forest products, and timberland assets."

The immediate callouts to the above direct quote are usually – "Office Max did a monetized Installment Sale and publicly announced it?" followed by "I thought this program was for Farmers?"

So– the direct wording from IRC 453a(b)3 cites exceptions to the Pledge Rule as property used in the production, trade, or business of Farming as defined by 2032A(e)(4), which further cites the definitions of "Farms" and "Farming Purpose." The IRS is usually quite helpful in providing definitions for every precise detail, which is terrific but beyond the scope of this eBook to transcribe.

Rather than give direct definitions, we will simply observe that directly according to the IRS, "Farming" includes "greenhouses, plantations, fur-bearing animals, agricultural or horticultural commodities and woodlands and more!

"Farming Purpose" includes "handling, drying, packing, grading or preparation for the market" and more!

Now we know that a legitimate Monetized Installment Program for 'Farmers' is available, and we now have a clue as to how complex it can be.

It is time to outline exactly how Q Financial and CB Farmers Trust were able to put a program like this together for the real farmers and farms of America, and not just the large companies that can afford the team of legal advisors!

Let's frame the program by stating that the system really resembles a mortgage loan with a first and second note built into the purchase on the surface. Think about that while we describe how it actually works.

Below is a diagram of the CB Farmers Trust Delaware Statutory Trust Program in action— I promise it feels less complex than it looks. Once the CB DSTP is deployed, all that happens is the farmer receives a semi—annual check for interest that is then used to make a semi—annual interest payment to the bank.

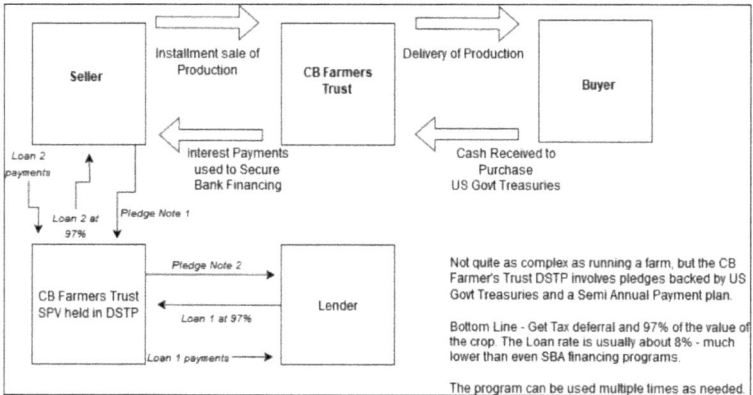

All that happens is a farmer sells the crop or farm to CB Farmers Trust for a note. CB Farmers Trust then collects from the buyer and holds all proceeds in US Govt Treasuries. Those Treasuries pay an interest payment to CB Farmers Trust, which forwards those payments back to the Farmer.

That is pretty simple. We call that the "Face Transaction," and it closely resembles buying a house and applying for credit with a Mortgage Lender, with the house being purchased used as collateral.

Behind the Face Transaction is an agreement to Fund the CB Farmers Trust Delaware Statutory Trust with the Promissory Note from CB Farmers Trust, that is Pledge #1. The Delaware Statutory Trust in the Farmer's name then pledges that same note to a Lender as part of Pledge #2. The Lender takes that same note and issues a 97% Loan to Value back to the CB DSTP, which forwards those proceeds back to the Farmer minus a 1% origination fee.

Out of pocket to the Farmer is $0 to deploy this tax advantage.

It is really no different in function than when your mortgage servicer changes, except you are seeing the rules that allow for the layered pledging of promissory notes from behind the stage.

The Wizard Behind the Curtain is that the Pledge rule can allow for changes in Lender / Loan Servicer at any time without triggering a change in Disposition of the Sold Asset (which causes a Gains Tax liability) as per Rev Rulings 82-122 and 75-457 respectively. This means that one single Promissory Note can move around almost anywhere behind the scenes.

CB Farmers Trust takes advantage of the Pledge Rule qualifiers and further uses a Master Trust Structure to hold the Assets that the lender wants to see backing the sale...which is a portfolio of US government treasuries, and that same Master Trust also functions as a Non-Related Party to maintain IRC 453 Installment Method requirements!

So- Complex but not overly complex, as streamlined as can be made to bring the tax benefits down to a level never achieved before.

The Interest rate charged is covered in part and even mostly offset by the Interest Payments of the US Govt Treasuries that are securing the Loan. CB Farmers Trust and the Lender are all paid by up- charging the Interest charged to the Farmer...and there is also a one-time origination fee of 1% - again, just like a mortgage.

With this tool, a qualifying Farm or Farmer now has a choice to allow this year's product really to finance next year's production and the rates offered are far lower than traditional loans because the portfolio of US Government Bonds offsets the finance charge.

The Government tax bill actually mostly pays for itself!

THE CHARITABLE REMAINDER TRUST

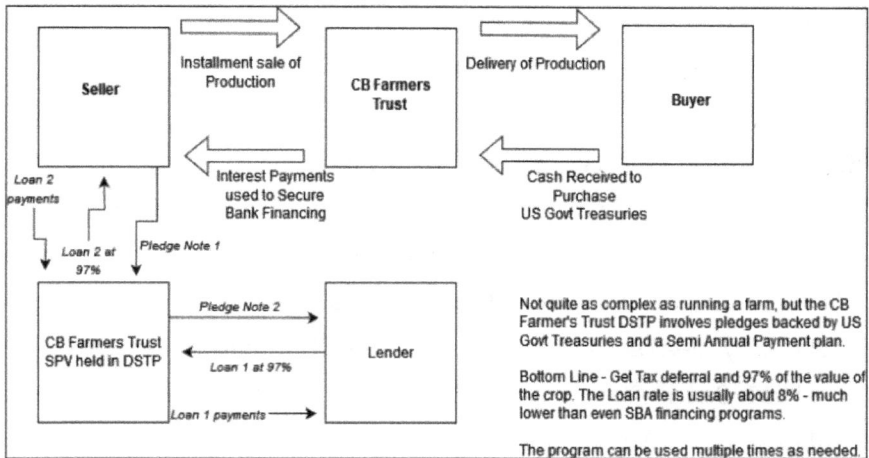

Charitable trusts of all types would require far more time to examine than this eBook can reasonably offer. Therefore, keep in mind that the explanations offered in this eBook are designed to be very broad. When fully investigating charitable gifting programs, please use a qualified advisor and take some time to read up on available literature from a variety of sources. There are a great many ways and a great many State-Specific rules for Charitable Gifting that dictate exactly what sort of controls the Grantor(s) retain and what sort of Charitable work may be supported through a Gift. This eBook does not cover any of those restrictions and will only offer a high topography overview of the concepts behind different allowable gifting structures.

Be warned! It is often simply easiest to use a well-known public charity for a Gift Annuity or Pooled Income Fund, but easy often leaves a lot of capability off the menu and can cause unforeseen issues that are important to know about for an Irrevocable election.

When a charitable trust is created, one is actually creating a legal charity. Surprising? Charitable trusts that are properly created are covered under section 501c(3) of the Internal Revenue Code. This is the section that specifically deals with Charities. A Charity is not subject to Capital Gains Tax and is also not subject to depreciation recapture tax. This means that those tax liabilities are effectively removed from consideration permanently if the Trust is funded with appreciated and depreciated assets. It also means that once created, a Charitable Trust may be used for multiple Gifts.

Charitable Trusts are irrevocable non-grantor trusts, meaning that the grantor (or the person making the gift) does not retain many rights concerning the use of the money or asset gifted to charity. Use of a third-party trustee is very common, though not always required (but usually strongly encouraged!).

Rather than go into too much detail, let me just mention

certain items the grantor of a charitable trust CAN normally control;

1. The amount of the future gift and, subsequently, the amount of the present tax deduction.

2. A well-structured trust will allow for multiple charities to be selected and will also allow the grantors to change which charities receive the future gift.

3. Grantors of a charitable trust also can stipulate how much money the trust pays them and for what length of time.

4. Grantors can also spell out how their gift to charity is to be used by that charity to a certain degree.

Now, the important thing to remember with charitable gifting is that you do not want to be too creative with your trust. If the charitable trust is disqualified, then there can be a ton of problems. The intent, after all, is to make a gift to charity, the key word being 'gift.'

Charitable gifting is encouraged by the government (Tax Deductions) and is actually one of the oldest strategies created. All forms of charitable gifting rely heavily upon calculating the actual amount of the gift to charity.

Therefore, the most important aspects of a Charitable Remainder Trust are based on the "present value of the future gift to charity." Since we are dealing with a future gift that occurs at the demise of the grantors with a Charitable Remainder Trust, mortality is the next most important consideration.

This is a long way of saying that generally, the older you are, the greater your tax deduction, but the amount of your tax deduction is also influenced by how much income the trust pays you while you are still alive.

Let's touch briefly on the different ways a grantor can be paid by creating a Charitable Remainder Trust. There are different flavors of a Remainder Trust that are all based on how the Grantor receives income. There are CRITs (Interest Trusts), CRATs (Annuity Trusts), CRUTs (UniTrust), and possibly Nim–CRUTs (Net Income Makeup Trusts).

A Charitable Remainder Annuity Trust will make a fixed payment based on the original gift amount for as long as the grantor is alive or for a specific term, for example, 20 years. This technique often allows for the largest tax deduction as well as a reasonable income paid to the grantor.

A Charitable Remainder Interest Trust will pay the grantor any interest or dividends earned but will not touch the original gift. This technique for determining income frequently means that the income the grantor receives from the trust will often fluctuate. This type of payment is the second most popular for owners of rental or investment property; essentially, the grantor still receives the same income from an income-producing property while making a charitable gift, receiving a tax deduction, and removing the asset from the taxable estate.

A Charitable Remainder Uni Trust will make a fixed payment percentage determined by the grantor and will pull money from both interest and principal to make that payment percentage. This type of payment structure is also popular as the expected income received by the grantor is relatively stable. Frequently, the owner of an investment property may be able to increase the income received from the gifted property, receive a tax deduction, and remove the asset from the taxable estate.

A Net Income Make-Up Charitable Remainder Trust allows for irregular payments to the grantor specifically requested when the trust is drafted. For example, one or more of the above payments are held aside by the trust and not actually paid to the grantor until the grantor requests it. Basically, this technique creates a "fund" accessible to the grantor when money is needed rather than always making payments.

Payments made to a grantor by any form of a Charitable trust are taxed as income, which can sometimes be a concern for individuals expecting to be in a high marginal tax bracket. This is also an important consideration for folks who are subject to the Alternative Minimum Tax, but there are ways to address this.

A grantor of a charitable trust, unlike some other Trusts, may be a legal entity and does not have to be a natural person. This means that a business entity may be allowed to create a charitable trust with certain restrictions.

If a business like an LLC creates a charitable trust, the income paid by the trust to the LLC may be used for business purposes and may allow for acceptable deductions. Likewise, this income may also be used to fund a retirement plan for the business owners or employees, which allows for a deferral on income tax. It is very important to review a strategy like this with a qualified tax advisor and attorney to learn all of the limitations of this particular technique.

You can probably understand at this point just how complex the topic of Charitable Gifting can be. A Charitable Remainder Trust is just one version of charitable gifting.

Since the point of this eBook is to expose a reader to a variety of Capital Gains Tax strategies, let's explore some of the other charitable gifting techniques after our case study.

Charitable Trust Case Study

Marcus is 67 years old, and he is ready to retire. Marcus has owned and managed a small apartment complex for more than 35 years. He has no kids, and his wife passed away three years ago. Over the course of 35 years, Marcus has depreciated his apartment building to zero. His Capital Gains Tax and Depreciation Recapture costs will be very large. After consulting with his team of advisors, Marcus feels most comfortable using a Charitable Remainder Trust to provide him with income during his retirement years based on the full sale price rather than having to pay the tax.

Since Charitable Trusts do not pay tax on gains and are not forced to recapture depreciation costs, Marcus will truly have the most money working for him by using this strategy. The trust is structured to pay Marcus an income for as long as he is alive, after which the charity will be able to claim the trust assets.

There are many different types of Charitable Trusts, and many are available in a pre-packaged format just by contacting your favored charity. Hiring a qualified financial advisor to manage the trust assets frequently allows for a higher income stream paid by the trust to the donor and greater control in selecting a charity.

It has been our experience that Charitable Trusts are more frequently used in combination with other strategies to help mitigate a tax bill. This is especially true with an individual or family selling many properties over the course of time. A Charitable Trust is often only used for one or two properties out of every four or five...usually the ones that have been depreciated the most.

Charitable Trusts can be used with property, but problems can arise from gifting 'encumbered' property. This means if you have a mortgage outstanding on a property, you almost certainly must be able to pay it off before a charitable gift occurs. While Split Interest Gifts are allowable and also further explained in a few more pages, those structures are very complex as they attempt to take a single Capital Asset and divide up equity and debt. Split Interest Gifts tend to be more expensive in design and administration and have extra challenges to overcome in the event of an audit.

Charitable Trusts can address both Capital Gains Tax and estate tax. When a charitable trust is deployed, it almost always turns a tax liability into a tax advantage in a number of different ways. When combined with a Life Insurance Settlement Trust, it is a powerful technique to sell a property in a tax- advantaged fashion.

Marcus' Charitable Remainder Trust Details:

Marcus bought a small apartment complex about 35 years ago with money he inherited. The purchase price was $300,000.00. It generates about $12,000.00 a month gross currently (20 units at $600.00 per month) and has no existing loans. The sales price is estimated at $2.5 Million.

	NORMAL SALE	MODEL Q™ STRUCTURED INSTALLMENT SALE	PRO/CON
SALE PRICE	$2.5 Million	$2.5 Million	
TAX OWED	$534,600.00	None	Charities are not subject to Capital Gains Tax. There is a further deduction of about $1,250,000.00 that Marcus can use.
DEPRECIATION RECAPTURED?	Yes, estimate $75,000.00	None	Charities are not subject to depreciation recapture costs.
AMOUNT RECEIVED FROM SALE	About $1,890,400.00 after tax. This would create about $113,424.00 annual income at 6% without depleting the principal.	Income payments would be a minimum of $125,000.00 per year and could be much higher	Higher payments are structured to last for as long as Marcus is alive.
HOW DOES IT AFFECT THE ESTATE?	The $1,965,400.00 is in the Estate.	The full $2.5 Million is removed from the estate. At death, the charity receives the trust balance.	

The bottom line is that a CRT is one of the oldest techniques to exchange an asset for a lifetime income. The only downside is that any heirs are cut out from whatever is gifted to the charity. This can be addressed through life insurance, which will pay a tax-free lump sum to heirs. When you add in the Tax Deduction for the gift, this is the only strategy that can change a tax liability into a tax advantage.

THE CHARITABLE LEAD TRUST

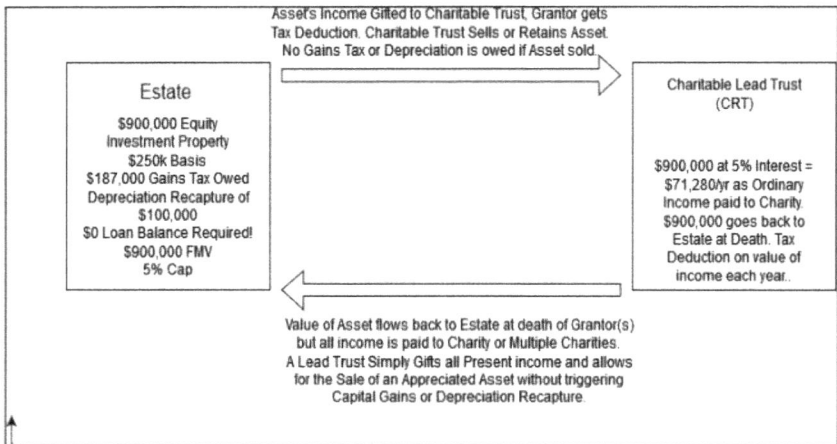

Asset's Income Gifted to Charitable Trust, Grantor gets Tax Deduction. Charitable Trust Sells or Retains Asset. No Gains Tax or Depreciation is owed if Asset sold.

Estate

$900,000 Equity
Investment Property
$250k Basis
$187,000 Gains Tax Owed
Depreciation Recapture of
$100,000
$0 Loan Balance Required!
$900,000 FMV
5% Cap

**Charitable Lead Trust
(CRT)**

$900,000 at 5% Interest =
$71,280/yr as Ordinary
Income paid to Charity.
$900,000 goes back to
Estate at Death. Tax
Deduction on value of
income each year..

Value of Asset flows back to Estate at death of Grantor(s) but all income is paid to Charity or Multiple Charities. A Lead Trust Simply Gifts all Present income and allows for the Sale of an Appreciated Asset without triggering Capital Gains or Depreciation Recapture.

The Charitable Lead Trust is basically the opposite of the Remainder Trust. In a Remainder Trust, the Income is paid to the Grantor, and the Asset goes to Charity. In a Lead Trust, the roles are reversed. The Income is paid to Charity while the Asset goes back into the Estate at the Death of the Grantor(s) and is passed to beneficiaries.

Just to make it easy for a Lead trust, we will use the same example as the Remainder Trust, Marcus.

Marcus is 67 years old, and he is ready to retire. Marcus has owned and managed a small apartment complex for more than 35 years. He has no kids, and his wife passed away three years ago. Over the course of 35 years, Marcus has depreciated his apartment building to zero. His Capital Gains Tax will be very large. After consulting with his team of advisors, Marcus feels most comfortable using a Charitable Lead Trust. He feels as if he has plenty of money to retire with, and he would really like to see several charities using his money while he is still alive. Marcus also finds tremendous satisfaction in being invited to Board meetings and sponsoring specific Charitable endeavors. Marcus also finds it deeply satisfying to influence and witness results directly

Though Marcus has no kids, he is very fond of his nephew and would like to retain part of his estate to pass to his brother's son.

Since Charitable Trusts do not pay tax on gains, and they are not forced to recapture depreciation costs, Marcus will truly have the most amount of money working for his Charitable Inclinations. The Lead Trust is structured to allow Marcus to pay various charities of his choice for as long as he is alive, after which the Value of the Trust will be made available to Marcus's favorite nephew.

The types of income paid to a Charity by a Lead Trust are essentially the same as with a Remainder Trust.

A Charitable Lead Annuity Trust will make a fixed series of payments to a charity for a specified period of time.

A Charitable Lead Interest Trust will pay a Charity interest earned on trust assets but will not touch the principal.

A Charitable Lead Uni Trust will make payments to a Charity from both principal and interest.

Each year that a qualified Charity receives income from a Lead Trust, the Grantor(s) receive a tax deduction.

We most frequently see Lead Trusts created by highly affluent individuals and families that do not really need extra income and would like to see the impact of their philanthropic efforts while they are alive. We also find Lead Trusts used by families that are accustomed to tithing to their church.

OTHER TYPES OF CHARITABLE GIFTING

There are many other charitable gifting techniques, but they are not as common as the Remainder and Lead Trusts when dealing with an appreciated asset.

A Pooled Income fund (aka Donor—Advised Fund) is a fund operated by a Charity for the benefit of folks seeking to have a no—hassle version of a Remainder Trust. The paperwork for the future gift and current income paid to the grantor is greatly simplified, but a significant amount of control is lost. All things considered, a Pooled Income Fund is probably the easiest way to make a charitable gift of an appreciated asset while still receiving an income, but the Grantors will not be able to change the charitable beneficiary of their gift or moderate income received.

Most Charitable entities have their own Pooled Income Fund, and if you are not very concerned about how your gift is to be used or if you do not want to support multiple charities, it is worth investigating.

A Family Foundation is another alternative, but it is not as common. Primarily used for highly affluent families, it would be rare to see a Foundation that was managing assets of less than four million dollars. If a Remainder

Trust was a sole proprietorship, then a Foundation would be a C-Corporation. Like a Remainder Trust, an asset is gifted into a Foundation account, and then the family meets periodically to discuss which Charities to support. There is a Board of Directors, minutes for meetings, and usually a salary paid to the family members 'employed' by the Foundation. Even with all of the extra work a Family Foundation requires, it is a great opportunity for a large family to meet consistently for a common goal. It is also a unique way to keep the family members of influential persons relatively out of the public spotlight.

A Quick Dialogue on Split-Interest Gifts

Often, a family or an owner of property is reluctant to give the entire value of an asset to a charity or a charitable trust. It is "possible" to perform a split-interest gift, which would allow a seller of property to identify what amount of an asset is gifted rather than gifting the whole asset.

Split Interest Gifting seems to be challenged successfully even more than charitable techniques, probably due to the fact of its complexity. Remember, you cannot gift encumbered property to a Charity; you have to pay off any Loans first, and you cannot normally receive a tax deduction for the Gift of 'Rent' for a property you own, especially if you are closely connected to the leadership of the Charity…yet these two facts seem to cause the most interest in designing a Split Interest Gift. Those types of

Split Interest Gifts do not tend to survive any scrutiny.

When Split Interest Gifts DO work, it means that charitable gifting can be pretty flexible. This topic is best illustrated by its own brief case study to demonstrate what it can accomplish.

Mildred is 75 and has no children, nor is she married. She is a retired social worker who created her own non-profit organization to assist victims of domestic abuse some years ago. Mildred owns a 4-plex apartment building she purchased in the late 70s, which is totally paid off and generates rental income of about $60,000.00 per year, which she uses to supplement her pension. Mildred wants to sell her 4- plex and use the money to fund a Charitable Remainder Trust that will benefit the non-profit she helped create.

The only problem is that Mildred would also like to see the benefit of the money she is dedicating to her cause rather than have the bulk of the gift occur after her death. A Split-Interest Charitable Remainder UniTrust (CRUT) is explored and compared to a regular sale as well as a non-Split Interest CRUT.

	NORMAL SALE	CRT	50% SPLIT INTEREST CRT	PRO/CON
SALE PRICE	$1.4 Million	$1.4 Million	$1.4 Million	
TAX OWED	$340,200.00	None	$170,100.00.	No Gains Tax. Split Interest Gifts must be correctly structured
CHARITABLE DEDUCTION	NONE	Between $280,000.00 and $700,000.00, depending on the Trust structure and age of the grantor.	Between $140,000.00 and $350,000.00 depending on the Trust structure and age of the grantor.	Smaller Deduction but more cash out of sale that is freely available.
AMOUNT RECEIVED FROM SALE	About $1,059,800.00 after tax creates $63,588.00 annual income at 6% without depleting principal..	Annual income payments would be a minimum of $70,000.00 per year and could be as high as $112,000 very easily.	Annual income payments between $35,000.00/yr and $56,000.00/ yr very easily. In addition, Mildred has $529,900.00 cash to spend however she chooses.	CRUT income is usually 5%-8% / yr
HOW DOES IT AFFECT THE ESTATE?	The $1,059,800.00 is in the Estate.	The full $1.4 Million asset is removed from the estate.	$700,000 is removed from the estate, and the after-tax amount of about $529,900.00 is included in the estate.	

The bottom line is that a Split Interest Gift can help manage taxes in a precise fashion, and a Charitable Deduction can help offset Capital Gains Taxes incurred from the amount of the asset retained by the seller. In this example, Mildred gets a reduced tax bill, approximately the same cash flow, and about $500,000.00 cash out of the deal to enjoy. Now, a note of caution: a Split Interest Gift to Charity must be performed in a certain way, and qualified legal and tax advice is highly recommended. The risk of having a Split Interest Gift to Charity be disqualified is greater than with a traditional gift to charity.

GRANTOR TRUSTS AND INTENTIONALLY DEFECTIVE GRANTOR TRUSTS

Earlier in this eBook, we mentioned these types of trusts as tools to help a property owner realize the biggest savings from the sale of a property. Well, this is true, but these techniques have very few advantages for Capital Gains Taxes. Indeed, the main advantage of most of these Irrevocable Grantor Trusts is the ability to keep an asset in the family while still providing for the support or income needs of the owner. How this works is that the 'seller' of the property creates a bona-fide and completed sale for a 'future interest' in the property while retaining some form of 'present interest' or income.

Frequently, trusts of this nature fall under the "Special Needs" category of this eBook as their main value is found in freezing the value of an estate or allowing for increased gifting of assets to the next generation.

The catch for Capital Gains Tax issues lies in the fact that you are performing a completed sale, and Capital Gains Tax will be owed, but in some cases, it is split between the buyer (children or relations commonly) and the seller if the transaction causes a change in the disposition of the appreciated asset. These types of trusts are generally not used if the asset is highly appreciated for this

reason, but they remain excellent candidates for concerns such as Medicare planning or reducing a potential estate tax through a structured gifting program to heirs.

HOW OFFSHORE GAINS TAX STRATEGIES ARE SUPPOSED TO WORK

There is quite a bit of misunderstanding regarding the technique to hold assets offshore, but the truth is that it is a very legal way to own assets. However, for the United States' compliant tax advantages, there are guidelines that must be followed.

Offshore tax-advantaged structures were originally created to allow a United States Insurance Company the ability to collect insurance premium payments abroad and not be subject to multiple layers of income taxes.

In the present day, the idea behind going 'offshore' is generally for asset protection purposes. It is safe to say that assets held properly offshore can be much harder to litigate against by the US Legal system. Why is this? Well, the US Court system will have limited jurisdiction over foreign powers, sometimes very little jurisdiction at all. Essentially, a few extra hoops are put in place that make assets held offshore harder to get to and generally more expensive to pursue.

However, since this eBook only discusses tax-advantaged techniques to sell property or a business, we will only focus on that segment of an offshore strategy.

It may not need to be said, but to have a tax advantage in the United States, you have to follow the United States tax law. This is the area that gives many offshore strategies a bad reputation because the reporting guidelines for US-compliant tax savings are very clear; however, the temptation to misrepresent the required reporting has caused many problems in the past.

You have to follow the rules if you choose an offshore strategy for either asset protection or tax advantages. After the Patriot Act was passed, the rules were basically stated as "do not try to hide assets offshore and accurately report assets held offshore. Pay taxes that are owed from any offshore accounts." If you follow the rules, you may still be audited, but you should not be penalized. The benefits can include tax advantages for your Tax strategy as well as adding another layer of foreign law to help protect those offshore assets.

Now, there are really only two US Compliant structures for tax advantages regarding assets held offshore. Since Offshore Tax Laws were written for Insurance Companies, it should not surprise you to learn that insurance vehicles like Variable Annuities (VAs) and Variable Universal Life Insurance (VULS) are the main choices for a tax-advantaged offshore asset.

(Note: the very same tools we are discussing for Offshore can also be held domestically through Captive Insurance Companies; the rules are the same. However, as promised, we are here to share with you how Offshore Tax Advantages are supposed to work! The author lists Captive Insurance as more of a contractual Tax advantage, right alongside Self-Directed Roth IRAs and Self-Directed Roth 401ks, which also achieve similar results once you solve the problem of getting the Asset into the Shelter.)

The main difference between VAs and VULs that you would buy from a financial advisor versus those that are created for offshore assets is very similar to the difference between having an IRA at a bank that you use for a mutual fund versus having a Self-Directed IRA that allows you to own investment property. The variable annuity or variable universal life insurance you hold through an offshore trust can be invested in virtually anything. When it does so, the future growth can be tax deferred, and the income can even be tax-free.

Now, the technique of going offshore is very complex; entire books can and have been dedicated to that sole subject. Instead of any further background information, let's explore two different case studies and then summarize key points.

Case Study #1 – Offshore and Tax Deferred until Withdrawn.

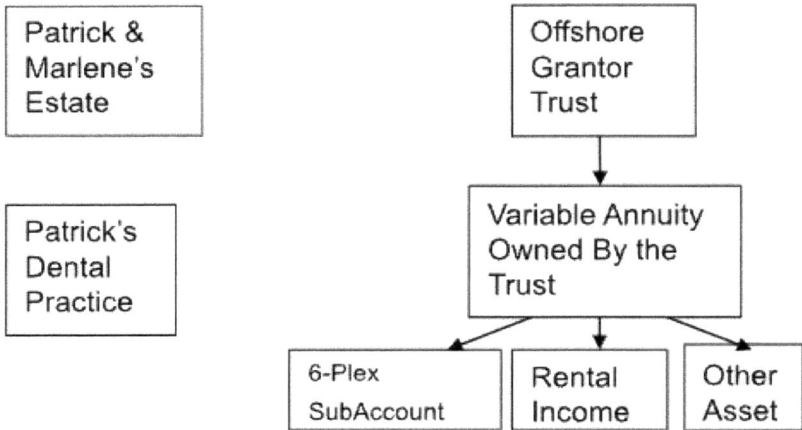

Patrick & Marlene's Estate		Offshore Grantor Trust

↓

Variable Annuity Owned By the Trust

Patrick's Dental Practice	

6-Plex SubAccount	Rental Income	Other Asset

Patrick and Marlene are both 54 years old. Patrick is a successful dentist who owns the commercial building used for the practice. Marlene is a fundraiser for a national non-profit company. They are accustomed to an annual income of about $300,000 from both of their jobs and are beginning to look forward to a possible early retirement. They have three children, the youngest of whom is still in college. Patrick's mother just died and left a 6-plex multi-unit apartment to Patrick and Marlene.

In this instance, Patrick and Marlene are primarily interested in tax advantages and future retirement since they are in the highest marginal tax bracket between federal and state taxes. They do not really need the income from the multi-unit they are considering selling and would like to keep the building since it has been in the family for years.

One of the techniques that are approached is an off-shore structure to continue owning the 6-plex building, primarily because the asset has just received a step-up in basis due to the death of Patrick's mother. This technique can defer income taxes from the rental income of the multi-unit until that income is needed, as well as avoid Capital Gains Taxes if the building were to be sold in the future. In addition to the tax benefits, depending on what foreign jurisdiction governs the asset, there could be additional legal hurdles to overcome in the event of a lawsuit or bankruptcy.

To accomplish the Offshore ownership, generally, a Grantor Trust is created and domiciled in a foreign country. This places the legal jurisdiction in the country that is selected as opposed to the United States. Furthermore, the Trustee of the Grantor Trust is usually also a foreign national, again to place legal jurisdiction outside of the US. The Grantor is usually offered some Rights to Income or Use without being offered complete Ownership or Control.

This is the typical structure of Offshore ownership.

Now, to get the tax advantage of tax-deferred growth through a variable annuity, Patrick and Marlene found a self-directed insurance company that is US-compliant. This means that actual insurance is provided, calculated, and charged (generally at the lowest acceptable standard). Furthermore, one of the sub-accounts in the CIC or Private Placement Variable Annuity policy becomes the 6-plex multi-unit building.

Getting the 6-plex into this structure requires a completed sale and formal change of ownership. This works very well for Patrick and Marlene since they just inherited the property and have little to no taxable gain.

This is a quick chart of the re-assignment of the 6-Plex building into the Offshore Structure. This structure is not owned in Patrick and Marlene's name and can be used to hold any number of assets. As the 6-plex earns rental income, that rental income can be invested in nearly any type of investment. As long as Patrick and Marlene do not receive the income themselves, taxes are deferred while the money is still fully available if needed.

The downsides with this technique of owning an asset are the same with any other Grantor Trust. If you already have a highly appreciated property, then this technique will do nothing to address the current tax liability. Also, as previously stated, there are additional tax forms to report to the US, which are generally handled by the offshore legal team that helps you create this structure. There is also a cost associated with the ongoing legal work to maintain a structure like this; all of these considerations and more should be examined before engaging in going "Offshore." (For example, in this illustration, Patrick and Marlene may be penalized if any money was withdrawn from this Offshore Asset until they hit the age of 59 ½ under US tax law governing Annuities.)

A serious downside to consider is that if everything is not done correctly with an Offshore Structure and you are audited, then the penalties are your own to bear, regardless of who was at fault. Remember to accurately disclose everything owned Offshore to file all of the correct tax forms and be wary of anyone who advises you to do otherwise behind closed doors.

The benefits are, simply put, tax-deferred growth of the appreciation of the 6-plex building as well as tax deferral on rental income generated. Basically, this asset has been turned into a retirement account for Patrick and Marlene without forcing a sale to a third party. As another consideration, due to Patrick's thriving dental practice, there may be substantial legal hurdles to overcome to tap the Asset value held offshore in the event that Patrick and Marlene were the subject of a lawsuit.

Case Study #2 Offshore and Tax-Free

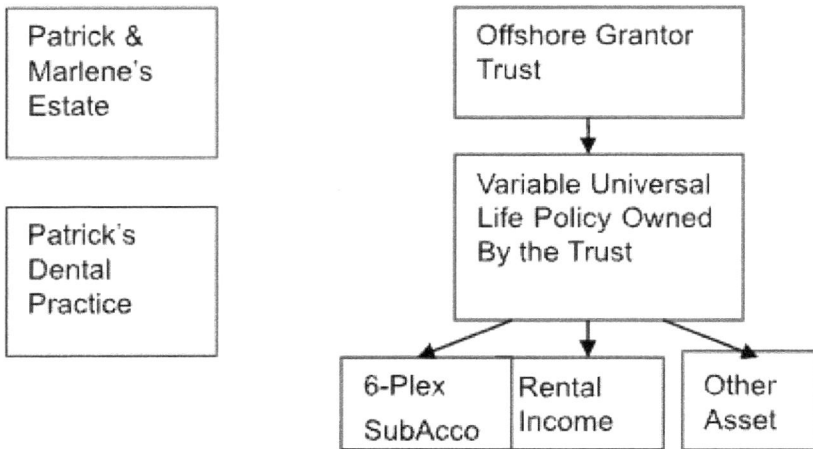

```
┌─────────────┐        ┌──────────────────┐
│ Patrick &   │        │ Offshore Grantor │
│ Marlene's   │        │ Trust            │
│ Estate      │        └──────────────────┘
└─────────────┘                 │
                                ▼
┌─────────────┐        ┌──────────────────┐
│ Patrick's   │        │ Variable Universal│
│ Dental      │        │ Life Policy Owned │
│ Practice    │        │ By the Trust      │
└─────────────┘        └──────────────────┘
```

6-Plex SubAcco	Rental Income	Other Asset

Let's go back to Patrick and Marlene and look at a slightly different approach that is available for their 6-plex building owned Offshore.

Instead of using a self-directed Variable Annuity policy, let's look at a self-directed Variable Universal Life Insurance policy. It is exactly the same structure as the previous case study. However, the tax advantages are completely different.

We have essentially the same Offshore Structure as before, with a few key differences. The cost of insurance can be greater with a VUL policy as compared to the mortality and expense charge by the VA in the previous example. Likewise, in a VUL, the idea is not to provide income; it is really better designed to pass wealth to the next generation with one key caveat. Policy loans from the self-directed VUL policy are tax-free, but they are loans, and they affect the future death benefit of the policy to the heirs.

Without going into any further detail, in this structure, it would be possible for Patrick and Marlene to keep the 6-plex building and have access to the rental income tax-free. If the 6-plex were to sell in the future, Capital Gains Tax would, again, not be a concern, and the policy would hold cash, and that cash could be used to purchase another suitable asset. The best use for this version of an Offshore Tax- Advantaged strategy would be if Patrick and Marlene wished to pass this 6-plex to their 3 children while still having access to rental incomes generated. Of course, the Offshore Entity will probably also have some additional protection from lawsuits, just like the previous example.

Offshore Structures can be viable strategies if they are approached with the right intent, and you have a good professional team to help you structure yours to the best effect.

OFFSHORE AND TAX ADVANTAGED BY TREATY

This eBook will not go into detail regarding tax treaties with foreign states and allowable structures and types of beneficial trade. These situations tend to be very time-specific in effectiveness and not pertinent to the average US Citizen.

This eBook is more concerned with US Tax Law and US Tax Structure exclusively; we leave these topics for discussion with qualified Attorneys while agreeing that such strategies do exist and are actually fairly common and highly complex as they deal with Foreign Law as well as US Law and can come and go as different jurisdictions seek to stimulate economy or trade.

BUSINESS EXIT STRATEGIES

Most of the tax-advantaged techniques covered in this eBook can also be used for the asset sale of a business. But before we examine how those strategies work, let's first take a look at the different ways to hold a business and structure a sale.

When considering taxation and how a business is held, essentially, you have two choices. Some sort of pass-through entity or a corporate structure is taxed at the corporate level and again down to employees.

If you are self-employed and manage a business through a sole proprietorship or a partnership, then you (and your partner) directly own both the assets and liabilities of your business.

In all other cases, it is important to note that you technically own the 'units' or 'shares' of the business, while the business entity itself owns the assets and liabilities of the business. This is important to note because it opens a few doors for a tax-advantaged transaction.

If you own a business in any form, it is always a good idea to consider how to sell or exit that business sometime down the road.

The two most common techniques for selling a business involve an Asset Sale or a Stock Sale. Stock sales primarily occur with businesses valued at over 25 million dollars, and even then, they occur infrequently. This is because when one sells a business as a stock sale, the buyer assumes both the assets and any present or future liabilities of that purchase. Naturally, this considerably slows down the due diligence part of the transaction as the buyer will seek to lessen or reduce the liability of the purchase.

For this eBook, our area of focus is on an Asset Sale.

It is always a good idea to spend a little money on a formal valuation and get feedback from a qualified professional on how to keep your books about one or two years prior to a sale, as this will help encourage a higher sale price or multiple.

When the sale occurs, there will almost always be a capital gain tax due for the asset sale component of the negotiated transaction. This is the same tax that a property owner experiences, and the same techniques to defer or avoid the Capital Gains Tax can be used.

Since a business sale is a negotiated process, frequently, a seller will be asked to "Carry a Note," which essentially means that the buyer will make ongoing payments for a period of time. This is especially true if any SBA funding is used, as the SBA typically funds to a maximum of 90%.

One of the techniques that can address this ongoing income is to change the terms so that the amount 'carried' by the seller is paid as a consulting fee. The seller of the business is then free to open a second company for the purpose of consulting and receive the payments as revenue. This allows for a variety of pretax techniques to shelter and tax defer the income. This technique is often used in conjunction with many of the capital gains deferral tools mentioned in this eBook.

As a perk for the buyer, since the payments are made as a consulting fee, those payments should probably be a deductible expense.

Another technique that is often used is to make the asset sale but leave the "sold" business operating. The monies that are paid to buy the assets are then technically revenue for the business. Again, this revenue can be used to declare income to any remaining employees and can then be placed into some sort of defined benefit retirement plan.

If a business is being sold to fund in part retirement, deferral of the tax in some form should be of great interest. Indeed, the basic idea of tax deferral is the cornerstone for retirement accounts.

The use of Defined Benefit plans or Deferred Compensation plans can be extremely beneficial. Business Owners will also want to understand the concept behind a 1042 Exchange, especially if part of the retirement strategy is to address estate tax concerns or if the sale is considered a reasonably profitable 'Family' business or Farm, although typically when one is selling intra-family, it gives rise to other gifting a sales strategies, the common would be the Family Limited Partnership aka "FLIP."

There are many caveats to using any of these strategies for a business sale, and the more time you spend with qualified professionals and asking questions, the better your outcome will be. All of your due diligence should begin before the business enters escrow and most definitely before a business closes escrow!

I think it is fair and reasonable to state that if you are planning on selling a business, the Exit Strategy process should take a year minimum, preferably two or three years. Why? Laying the proper foundation for a business sale can be as valuable as the actual sale in terms of controlling tax and establishing a more enticing profitability history to help increase your multiple.

Q Financial has experience with all forms of Business Sales, and the Model Q™ Installment Sale Trust has exceptional results in providing tax advantages to Asset based businesses, especially those that are Real-Estate heavy, such as Car Washes and Storage Units but even more surprisingly to Partnership interests such as often found in medical, dental or veterinary practice and Franchise routes as can be found with Fed Ex Route.

The Advanced Planning chapter in the planned book for Estate Planning discusses a variety of tax advantage techniques to sell real estate and business assets in a layered approach. More complex transactions for values typically over $4 Million dollars. There are also case studies for a property sale, but it is important to remember that in almost all cases, these same strategies can be used for a part business sale as well. The moving part to be aware of is what is considered an 'Asset" by the IRS, as assets held long-term generally have access to the Capital Gain strategies described in this eBook.

So, business owners have extra work cut out for them. The overall guidelines to keep the most of what you have earned from creating your business can be summarized as follows:

1. Starting years in advance, hire a business valuation expert and a consultant. Frequently small changes in record keeping and DECLARING PROFITS will increase your multiple and net you a higher sales price at the end of the day.

2. Consider your life plan and Income plan, taking hints from this eBook as to which strategies might help resolve any Capital Gains Tax on the asset portion of the sale. If estate tax is a concern, investigate gifting stock from your company BEFORE you sell when the value of the stock is lower. Options may also be deployed, which may allow for accelerated gifting upon a trigger event or a strike price in value is achieved.

3. Keep in mind that any carryback or portion of the sale you carry can be structured to not immediately be taxable. This can be achieved with all or a portion of the ongoing payments made to you by a buyer.

You will end up relying heavily on your team of professional advisors, but it will have a definite impact on the quality of a retirement funded by a business sale.

CLOSING STATEMENTS

Now, you should have a pretty good idea of many ways to sell a highly appreciated property or business in a tax-advantaged fashion. In addition to that, we have discussed not only techniques to address Capital Gains but also Depreciation Recapture. We have also introduced the Model Q™ Installment Sale Trust and the Model Q™ Investment Philosophy that we feel solves Income needs in a way that avoids systematic market risk that is different from other approaches.

We have hopefully explained why Model Q™, in particular, could have significant benefits for you, the reader.

We have covered how to determine your Life Plan or Goal after the transaction and how planning with the right professionals can influence and improve the effectiveness of your retirement strategy.

Perhaps this means you need to implement several strategies?

We have also discussed the changes in the financial industry over time, how many fallacies exist in modern advice, and how the structure of your professional services is more important than ever to be aware of.

Further details on how to bridge Capital Gains Tax advantages with Estate Planning and long-term Rights and Powers that may be retained through generations are explained in our next eBook on Estate Planning. Advanced Estate Planning frequently combines multiple strategies for effect over a longer period of time.

We have also discussed how to find, qualify, and manage a team of professionals from different areas of practice so that they work effectively on your behalf.

We at Qualified Financial truly hope this eBook has been helpful in explaining, conceptually, all of your tax strategy options! We also hope that the countless hours that were spent learning, designing, and applying these strategies are also apparent and that the experience demonstrated through this eBook helps to create additional trust in our competence.

Please give us a visit at www.Q-Financial.com a call 800-694-5133 or fill out a Proforma report request if you believe we can assist you in any fashion.

www.ingramcontent.com/pod-product-compliance
Lightning Source LLC
Chambersburg PA
CBHW060006210326

41520CB00009B/838